Dear Amy,
Best of luck in
all your efforts
on behalf of your
kids —
Joyce Cooper-Kahn

LATE, LOST, and UNPREPARED

A Parents' Guide to Helping Children with Executive Functioning

Joyce Cooper-Kahn, Ph.D.
Laurie C. Dietzel, Ph.D.

WOODBINE HOUSE 2008

Published in the United States of America by Woodbine House, Inc., 6510 Bells Mill
Rd., Bethesda, MD 20817. 800-843-7323. www.woodbinehouse.com

Library of Congress Cataloging-in-Publication Data

Cooper-Kahn, Joyce.
 Late, lost and unprepared / Joyce Cooper-Kahn, Laurie C. Dietzel.
   p. cm.
 Includes bibliographical references and index.
 ISBN 978-1-890627-84-3 (alk. paper)
 1. Executive ability in children. 2. Self-management (Psychology) for children. I.
Dietzel, Laurie C. II. Title.
 BF723.E93C66 2008
 649'.152--dc22

                                                                              2008032363

Manufactured in the United States of America

10   9   8

Joyce Cooper-Kahn
To my son, from whom I have learned, day by day,
about the struggles and triumphs of learning to
compensate for weak executive functioning

Laurie C. Dietzel
To my parents, Louise Dietzel and Sam Dietzel
(1936-2000), my husband, Claude Allen, and our
daughter, Emma Allen

TABLE OF CONTENTS

Part II: What You Can Do about It

Strategies to Help a Child with Written Expression and
      Other Complex, Multi-Step Tasks
Strategies to Help a Child Who Interrupts Others So She
      Won't Forget What She Wants to Say
Strategies to Help a Child Who Needs to Re-Read or Re-Learn
      Information – It Just Doesn't Stick
Strategies to Help a Child Who Has Trouble Taking Notes in Class
Case Study: Putting It All together
Transitioning From Short-Term to Long-Term Goals
Educate Others and Advocate for Your Child
Final Thoughts

Acknowledgements

Joyce Cooper-Kahn:

I want to thank my mother, Lenora Cooper, and my father, Solomon Cooper (1921-2007), who instilled in me a deep conviction that there is important, interesting work to be done in the world, and encouraged me as I discovered just what that meant for me.

I am overwhelmingly grateful for the love and support of my husband, Michael Kahn, who believes deeply in the process of reaching inward for strength as we seek to be our best selves.

Laurie Dietzel has been a wonderful co-author. Her sharp intellect and depth of knowledge proclaimed itself in a package that included just the right, wacky sense of humor to make it clear that we were sympatico from the start. The experience of writing together has been easier than I could have ever imagined.

Laurie C. Dietzel:

I am so privileged to work with Jamie Butler, my business partner and friend. I thank her for her abiding support, understanding, and encouragement. I would also like to thank Elaine Castles for sparking my interest in assessment and neuropsychology and for helping me learn so many important skills and lessons as a developing psychologist.

I also want to acknowledge my sisters, Rebecca Dietzel and Beth Martell, and my mother-in-law, Ruth Allen, for all of their support. I am also so fortunate to have the support of two amazing friends, Ellen Iscoe and Fran Rubinetti.

Last but certainly not least, I would like to thank Joyce Cooper-Kahn for inviting me to work on this project with her. This has been an amazing experience and I am grateful for her generosity in sharing her wisdom and expertise.

*   *   *   *   *

We want to thank our editors at Woodbine House for their skillful editing and warm, approachable style.

Both of us particularly acknowledge all the children and families who have contributed to this book by entrusting their care to us. The clinical practice of psychology is so much more than imparting knowledge to others or identifying and fixing problems. It is built on a reciprocal, trusting exchange, and we are so fortunate to learn from the individuals who have let us into their lives and allowed us to share in their struggles and their dreams.

Part 1
WHAT YOU NEED TO KNOW

1

Introduction

Matthew does all his homework, but half the time he still gets zeroes because he doesn't turn it in to the teacher.

Nikki seems so irresponsible in her work habits even though she wants to do well. How will she ever make it in the world? Help!

Every morning we have a major battle in our house. Alan's alarm goes off at quarter of seven. I have to remind him to get out of bed at least five times, and then I have to keep nagging just to get him to brush his teeth and get dressed before the bus comes. And he still misses the bus! I'm so tired of going through this every morning.

You should see Mary's backpack! Old papers, gum wrappers, homework assignments...what a mess! Her locker looks the same way. How can I help her get organized?

Sound familiar? All of these kids have problems with what professionals call "executive functioning." Sound like a confusing term? We agree. For now, think of executive functioning as the administrator and manager of a complex and busy system—the system of the human brain. (For more on how executive function is defined, read on to the next chapter.)

Some of the children in our examples may also have some specific disorder. If your child has an attention disorder, then these scenarios probably sound all too familiar. (In fact, many experts in the field suggest that AD/HD be reconceptualized as an "executive disorder.") However, kids with attention disorders are by no means the only ones that experience executive functioning problems. Problems with executive functioning are generic. Like a rash, executive dysfunction is a symptom that sometimes appears alone and sometimes is part of a larger problem. This broader diagnosis might be a learning disability (LD), autism spectrum disorder (ASD), or other condition, such as a range of neurodevelopmental, psychiatric, and medical disorders (more on this in Chapter 7).

Are there kids with no diagnosed disability who struggle with organization, planning, self-control, and time management? Absolutely! We see them in our offices all the time.

We have good news and bad news for you. Here's the good news: There are things you can do—interventions—that help. The interventions in this book are not specific to any disorder. They are designed to be helpful whether or not your child has been diagnosed with AD/HD, a learning disability, another developmental condition, or has no formal or specific diagnosis at all. Among those who work with kids with executive dysfunction, there is much accumulated wisdom and experience that can guide you as you work at your job of parenting a disorganized child.

Now the bad news: We do not have all the answers for you. We can make the job easier but we cannot make it easy.

Why Another Book?

If you are reading this book, chances are you are a parent or a teacher or other professional who works with kids. And there is also a good chance that you are frustrated and weary with the effort of trying to help your disorganized kid meet the demands of the world. You are also probably confused about how to help.

We wrote this book to provide practical information about the executive functions, a set of related yet distinct skills that serve as our organizers. These executive functions are complex, but we have faith in your ability to learn what you need to know to be helpful to the child or children you have in mind. You **need** to know this information if you are going to do your best as the parent or teacher or professional of a child who is relying upon you to help him grow up to be the best he can be.

We wrote this book because when we looked for good books or articles to recommend to our clients, what we found was quite unsatisfactory. Here's why: There is some information for professionals in the scientific literature, but many of the recommended strategies are so complex that they just seem impractical. Much of the information is also directed toward specific disorders, rather than looking at the problems common to all kids with organizational difficulties. There are some suggestions for helping disorganized kids in general parenting books, but we want to focus on just the information that you most need as the parent of a disorganized child.

Further, much of what is out there focuses on what you can do in the short-term to help your child through the day. But if all you are doing is getting your child through the day, then you are only doing half your job! Adults working with disorganized children also need strategies that help kids to be successful and independent in the long run.

Perhaps most importantly, we want to offer information that helps you understand the **process** of helping a child with executive dysfunction. Many books on study skills seem to assume that simply giving the child information on how to organize leads to improved daily performance. But in our experience, it's not that simple. We've seen that building better executive functioning occurs over time and most often requires ongoing practice and support.

Finally, so much of what is out there is so serious that it made us feel all "doom and gloom" when we read it. That just didn't fit with our experience of the positive qualities that can exist side by side with executive dysfunction. Executive functions—whether a strength or weakness—are not the total of a person! So we decided to write a basic guide that would provide:

- down-to-earth information;
- practical examples;
- perspective and a sense of humor;
- a framework of understanding that allows you to think on your feet; and
- strategies that address both your short-term and long-term goals for your child.

Who Are We?

We are both clinical psychologists in private practice. In our daily work we provide evaluations of children and adolescents with attention and learning problems, guidance for their parents, and school consultation regarding how to help facilitate these kids' development.

Through our work with children and adolescents, parents, and teachers, we have come to appreciate the importance of the executive functions in academic performance, social interactions, and coping with daily life. We value maintaining a sense of humor and reasonable perspective when dealing with these weaknesses, but we also know that executive function weaknesses can be a source of tremendous frustration and stress for kids, parents, and teachers.

We are also parents. Like you, we continue to experience the joy, the frustration, and the confusion that accompanies this job. Our children keep us humble. One of us has lived in the presence of males with executive dysfunction for most of her life (JCK). As the daughter, sister, and mother of successful men who struggle with executive dysfunction, she brings a personal, as well as professional, sense of passion and compassion to this work. The other (LD) approaches this book with great humility as her daughter is quite young and is teaching her more about parenting and child development than can be covered in any academic course. For both of us, it is the parents and the children that we see every day in our offices who have rounded out our personal experience and our book learning. These are not just abstract issues. These are issues that parents and kids struggle with every day. We hope that this guide helps you put your efforts where they will do the most good. We understand how much patience and flexibility is required to raise a child with executive weaknesses, and applaud you for hanging in there.

The Plan for This Book

We have organized this book in short chapters so that you can use it as a reference, one topic at a time. Parents are busy people and need practical information to help them feel more comfortable trusting their judgment when making parenting decisions.

Some of you reading these words now are going to read every single word in this book. For others (you know who you are) if you have read this whole introduction, it is likely the longest stretch of reading you are going to do! You are more likely to pick up this book when you are feeling desperate and look for a paragraph, a sentence, anything that helps you at that moment. We know all kinds of parents, and we appreciate all your different styles.

The book is divided into two main parts; the first contains what you need to know about executive functions, i.e., what they are, how you know if your child has weaknesses in these areas and why, the impact they have on daily life, family, and emotions, and the assessment process. The second part of this book—the meat—details what you can do to help your child with executive weakness, *including how to get in the right mind-set to best support your child now and in the future, and specific interventions for day-to-day struggles.*

The information in this book is, of course, applicable to all children and adolescents, boys and girls alike. To make the information more readable, we alternate the use of gender by chapter.

We hope that this book is useful to everyone and invite you to use the book however it makes sense to you. We're rooting for you all!

2

What Is Executive Functioning?

THE BASICS

➢ The executive functions all serve a "command and control" function; they can be viewed as the "conductor" of all cognitive skills.

➢ Executive functions help you manage life tasks of all types. For example, executive functions let you organize a trip, a research project, or a paper for school.

➢ Often, when we think of problems with executive functioning, we think of disorganization. However, organization is only one of these important skills.

The term "executive functioning" has become a common buzzword in schools and psychology offices. This is more than just a passing fad. In fact, neuropsychologists have been studying these skills for many years. We believe that the focus on executive functioning represents a significant advancement in our understanding of children (and adults!) and their unique profile of strengths and weaknesses.

A Formal Definition of Executive Functioning

Now (drum roll please), here is a formal definition of executive functioning:

The executive functions are a set of processes that all have to do with managing oneself and one's resources in order to achieve a goal. It is an umbrella term for the neurologically-based skills involving mental control and self-regulation.

What mental control skills are covered under this umbrella? Different researchers and practitioners have their own favorite lists, although the overall concept is basically the same. We use the list proposed by Drs. Gerard A. Gioia, Peter K. Isquith, Steven C. Guy, and Lauren Kenworthy. These psychologists developed their understanding of executive functions through sound research and created a rating scale that helps parents, teachers, and professionals understand a particular child and think more specifically about how to help. More on this is discussed later in this chapter.

Before looking at the list of specific characteristics encompassed by the broad category of executive functions, we'd like to provide an example that makes the concepts more concrete.

Understanding Executive Functions by Looking at Life without Them

Thinking about what life is like for someone with weak executive functioning gives us a better understanding of the way these core skills affect our ability to manage life tasks. In the interest of making the concepts immediately relevant and meaningful, our example focuses on an adult, since we assume that most people reading this book are adults, too. Throughout the rest of the book we've included mostly examples of executive functioning in younger people.

The Road Trip without a Map

We'd like to tell you a story about our friend, Robin, who lives life without the benefit of strong executive functioning. Robin is a composite of many individuals we have known, and she struggles with weaknesses in executive skills, despite her well-intentioned efforts to reform herself.

One day in May, Robin gets a phone call from her Aunt Sue in Merryville, Missouri. Aunt Sue is planning a family reunion in July, and she wants to know if Robin and her family can come. All of the extended family will be there. The little town will be overrun with relatives and it is going to be a great corralling of the family from all across the United States. Robin is excited at the prospect and eagerly says, "Of course we'll be there! We wouldn't miss it!"

Aunt Sue gives Robin all the particulars, including the dates of the reunion and places to stay. Robin rummages around in the kitchen junk drawer for a pencil while her aunt talks, but she never does find one with a point on it. She promises to herself to find a pencil and write down all the details just as soon as she gets off the phone. But by the time she hangs up, she can't remember the specifics. She makes a mental note to call back soon to get the dates.

That evening, Robin excitedly tells her husband and two children about the reunion. Her husband asks when it will take place. "Some time in July. I don't remember exactly." He says, "Well, please find out this week because I have to request vacation time at work." Their fifteen-year-old son exclaims, "Hey, I thought July was when I was supposed to go to Band Camp!" "Didn't you remember?" Robin's daughter practically shouts, "I'm going to Ocean City with Julie and her family sometime in July." Robin blows up at them all, yelling, "Why are you all being so negative? This is supposed to be fun!"

About once a week, Robin's husband reminds her to get the information about the reunion. She promises to do so. (And she really means to get around to it!) Finally, in June, Robin's husband gets very annoyed and says, "Do it now! I'm going to stay right here in the kitchen until you call!" Robin makes the call and gets the dates as well as the other particulars. Her husband harrumphs around the house the rest of the evening because now he has only three weeks left before the requested time-off. Luck is on their side, though, because he manages to arrange the vacation around work, and the reunion dates do not conflict with the kids' activities.

Over the next three weeks, thoughts about the trip float through Robin's head from time to time. She thinks about how the kids will need to have things to do in the car since it's a long trip. She thinks about taking food and snacks for the ride. She thinks about getting her work at the office cleared up in advance so she can be free of commitments for the vacation. She thinks, "I really should take care of that stuff."

A few days before it is time to leave for the two-day drive to Missouri, she starts piling stuff into the van, including clothes and other supplies. (You can only imagine what the inside of this van looks like!)

Finally, it's time to pile the people into the van, too. On the way out of the house, one of the kids asks, "Who will be taking care of the cats while we're gone?" Robin moans, "Oh no! I forgot about that. We can't just leave them here to die and there's no one to take care of them! Now we can't go. What will we tell Aunt Sue?" Her husband takes over, and starts calling around the neighborhood until he finds a teenager who can do the pet sitting. The crisis passes. The cats will be fine.

So, they're off. Robin's husband drives the first shift. He pulls out of the neighborhood, gets onto the main highway, and then asks, "So, what's the game plan? What's the route?" Robin answers, "Missouri is west, so I know we have to go west." He looks at Robin incredulously and says, "You don't know any more details than *that*? Well, get out the map. We can't just head west with no more information that that!" And, of course, Robin says, "What map? I don't have a map." Robin's husband sighs and shakes his head. "Oh no! Another road trip without a map! Why didn't you tell me you were having trouble getting it all organized? I could have helped." Robin replied, "I didn't have any trouble. Everything is fine. We're in the car, aren't we? We'll get there. What are you so upset about?"

Do you think Robin had made reservations for where to stay along the way? Do you think she had planned out how much cash they would need for the trip or made it to the bank ahead of time? These and many other details, of course, had escaped planning.

A List of Executive Functions

With this example as a base, let's turn back to the question of what specific abilities are covered under the umbrella term of executive functioning. Below is the list of executive functions from Dr. Gioia and his colleagues. We've included a specific illustration of each executive function from our case study of Robin in parentheses after each definition.

1. **Inhibition**—The ability to stop one's own behavior at the appropriate time, including stopping actions and thoughts. The flip side of inhibition is impulsivity; if you have weak ability to stop yourself from acting on your impulses, then you are "impulsive." (When Aunt Sue called, it would have made sense to tell her, "Let me check the calendar first. It sounds great, but

I just need to look at everybody's schedules before I commit the whole family.")

2. **Shift**—The ability to move freely from one situation to another and to think flexibly in order to respond appropriately to the situation. (When the question emerged regarding who would watch the cats, Robin was stymied. Her husband, on the other hand, began generating possible solutions and was able to solve the problem relatively easily.)

3. **Emotional Control**—The ability to modulate emotional responses by bringing rational thought to bear on feelings. (The example here is Robin's anger when confronted with her own impulsive behavior in committing the family before checking out the dates: "Why are you all being so negative?")

4. **Initiation**—The ability to begin a task or activity and to independently generate ideas, responses, or problem-solving strategies. (Robin thought about calling to check on the date of the reunion, but she just didn't get around to it until her husband initiated the process.)

5. **Working Memory**—The capacity to hold information in mind for the purpose of completing a task. (Robin could not keep the dates of the reunion in her head long enough to put them on the calendar after her initial phone call from Aunt Sue.)

6. **Planning/Organization**—The ability to manage current and future-oriented task demands. (In this case, Robin lacked the ability to systematically think about what the family would need to be ready for the trip and to get to the intended place at the intended time with their needs cared for along the way.)

7. **Organization of Materials**—The ability to impose order on work, play, and storage spaces. (It was Robin's job to organize the things needed for the trip. However, she just piled things into the car rather than systematically making checklists and organizing things so important items would be easily accessible, so the space would be used efficiently, and so that people and "stuff" would be orderly and comfortable in the car.)

8. **Self-Monitoring**—The ability to monitor one's own performance and to measure it against some standard of what is needed or expected. (Despite the fact that they're off to Missouri without knowing how to get there, with almost no planning for what will happen along the way, and without a map, Robin does not understand why her husband is so upset.)

The executive functions are a diverse, but related and overlapping, set of skills. In order to understand a person, it is important to look at which executive skills are problematic for her and to what degree. We will talk more about the assessment process in Chapter 6, but we want to point out here that there are rating scales that can be used to collect the observations of parents and teachers in order to create a child's "executive profile."

How This Book is Organized

This book addresses all of the executive functions listed by Dr. Gioia and his colleagues. For the sake of simplicity, we've combined functions that have similar interventions into single chapters in Part II of this book. For example, we merged two functions above—*Planning/Organization* and *Organization of Materials*—into one, Chapter 15: Helping Children Plan and Organize. The strategies detailed in the second half of this book will help children with:

- Impulse Control
- Cognitive Flexibility (changing and making transitions)
- Initiating (getting started)
- Working Memory
- Planning and Organization
- Self-Monitoring

Final Thoughts

Understanding a person's executive functioning abilities tells us about only one aspect of that person's profile, albeit an important one. However, knowing about an individual's executive skills does not tell us how smart or charming or verbally expressive that person is. Nor does it teach us about the person's musical and athletic abilities or temperament or a host of other important factors. While people with executive dysfunction share a weakness in the command-and-control system, they are as unique as the proverbial snowflake.

3

Development of Executive Functions

To set realistic expectations for our children, it is important to understand the typical, or expected, development of the executive functions. Just as we expect children to walk and talk by certain ages, we expect them to learn to plan, organize, and manage tasks more efficiently and independently as they get older.

The development of executive skills is related both to the biological process of brain maturation (nature) and experience (nurture). This development moves kids from dependence on adult-provided structure and support to more independent, flexible ways of thinking and acting. There is considerable variability in the rate at which children develop executive control. Some children experience delays in the development of these important skills. Some may catch up, while others continue to experience executive weaknesses as adults.

Simply put, the brain's frontal and prefrontal lobes are the primary "home" of executive function. Although these are not the only brain regions responsible for these mental control skills, the frontal lobes are the last to fully mature. The frontal and prefrontal areas usually achieve full development by the mid-twenties; but for people with delays in these areas, development continues into the early 30s!

There are many good books that lay out the complexities of neuro-anatomy and brain development. Because this discussion is not within the scope of this book, our reference list at the end of the book offers suggestions for books that do a great job of explaining the intricate balance between nature and nurture in this process.

Why Is My Child Having Problems with Executive Skill Development?

When parents first come to see us, they are often worried about what is causing their child's executive weaknesses and if they are to blame. Here are some of the questions we are frequently asked: "My wife is very disorganized; does this run in families?" "Does it mean my child is brain damaged if he has been diagnosed with executive dysfunction?" "When I was pregnant with Sara, I had an occasional cup of coffee. Could that have caused her problems?"

For most children with executive weaknesses, there is no known cause. We describe these as *developmental* weaknesses because there is no one identifiable event or factor that interfered with brain development. While modeling and teaching are important, it is important to remember that parents can do a fine job of providing what a child needs, and that child can still experience delays in development.

For most kids who experience executive function delays, these weaknesses are likely due to inefficient communication among brain regions rather than any overt, localized problems, such as damage in one specific area. We *do* know that exposure to alcohol, certain drugs, or toxins during pregnancy, as well as premature birth, are all risk factors for delays in cognitive development. Kids who experienced early abuse, neglect, or other traumatic experiences are also vulnerable to delays in development. We also know that executive weaknesses (related to AD/HD and learning disabilities) run in families, although we do not yet understand exactly how genetic transmission works (except for some genetic syndromes such as Turner syndrome, velocardiofacial syndrome, and fragile X syndrome). We also know that a disease process or injury to the brain may result in *acquired* executive dysfunction in kids who were previously developing typically.

I.Q. and Executive Functioning

Many people assume that people with strong intelligence naturally have good executive skills. We expect "smart" kids to also have strong work habits and the ability to easily manage daily demands at home and school. However, intelligence and executive skills are only moderately correlated. That means that a highly gifted student may experience below average impulse control, planning, and organizational skills. After all, the ability to intellectually analyze and understand a task does not mean that a child can efficiently get started on and complete the task. On the other end of the spectrum, although most people with significant mental retardation also have weak executive skills, we have met many kids who perform below average on I.Q. tests yet have good ability to learn routines and manage daily tasks.

Typical Development

The Preschool Years:

Infants and very young children "live in the moment" and push for immediate gratification of their needs and wants. Although one-year-olds begin to develop the ability to work towards a goal (e.g., "I want that toy"), they can often be distracted with the offer of something else that is appealing to them. They become more persistent as they begin to be better able to hold an idea in mind and to think beyond the distractions in their way. Toddlers usually remain quite impulsive, gradually increasing their abilities to make simple plans and organize their behavior and their play. To a great extent, this development mirrors the development of language, as words serve as the internal symbols that let the young child begin to think and plan. Most two- and three-year-olds are able to delay gratification for a few minutes to attain a goal.

> *Jimmy is a three-year-old who loves playing with his train set. However, he has learned that he has to get dressed and brush his teeth before playtime. Jimmy still needs to have a parent close by who provides reminders to follow the routine, which is age-appropriate. In contrast to most one-year-olds and some two-year-olds, he can often stay in control of his impulses long enough to complete the less desirable tasks in order to get to what he most wants to do.*

Elementary School:

Once a child enters school, he is subject to increasing demands for task completion and impulse control. Children whose executive skills are developing as expected begin to think more flexibly about solving problems, although they continue to be quite focused on the "here and now." As kids proceed through elementary school, they show steady development of their planning, organizational, and self-monitoring skills and become more efficient when completing work. Working memory (the ability to hold information and directions for a brief period of time) also continues to develop. It is reasonable to expect most second and third graders to be able to easily follow two- to three-step directions and to remain focused in class for relatively long periods of time. Many fourth and fifth graders are able to do a pretty good job organizing their notebooks, desks, and lockers, although they may still need reminders and "check-ins" from their parents and teachers.

> *Lance is a typical third grader. Although his ability to accurately record his homework assignments, complete in-class work independently, and get ready for school and bed is improving, he still needs reminders. Lance needs help a few times a week with organizing his backpack and cleaning his room and school locker. While he is becoming more independent with his daily homework, he still needs considerable assistance completing long-term projects and editing his written work.*

Middle School:

By about age eleven or twelve, most kids are able to independently manage the daily routine at home and at school. From about age ten on, the more complex executive skills play an increasing role and build upon the impulse control and basic task management skills that were developed at earlier ages. These include time management, sequencing more complex tasks, keeping track of lots of information at the same time, setting goals, and organizing tasks. Kids begin to be more effective at monitoring their own behavior and adjusting their approach when an initial attempt to complete a task is not successful.

Jenny is a seventh grader whose parents have noticed a big "jump" in her ability to manage her homework. She usually gets started on her own, does a good job completing the work accurately (and without rushing to finish), and has started to use a calendar to plan for tests and long-term projects.

In conjunction with the natural unfolding of development, even kids with normal executive functioning may need some help learning how to manage the increased demands of middle/junior high school. The change from one primary teacher to multiple teachers that generally occurs as children enter middle school requires increased organizational skills. Most students benefit from preparation before this transition and explicit instruction in how to keep track of assignments, effectively use a locker, and coordinate daily schedules.

High School:

During the high school years, growth occurs in the form of fine-tuning skills in independent planning and organization. For most students, work that once took considerable effort becomes more automatic and faster. Kids think much more flexibly (if their executive skill development is on track) and can manage more demanding academic work.

Rick is a fifteen-year-old who no longer needs reminders to complete his weekly chores or to pack up his equipment and be ready to leave for soccer practice on time. He has internalized the daily and weekly schedule, and although he is not consciously aware of it, now plans and organizes his days to include all that he needs and wants to do. The only times that he needs reminders and parental support are when he is overtired or at the end of the school semester during "crunch" time.

Research has shown that during adolescence, most kids demonstrate increasing ability to work more efficiently and handle complex demands and tasks. The demands increase accordingly. Because of the increased expectations, students with executive weaknesses need more external structure and support than they did in earlier grades. Of course, this needs to be provided in a sensitive way that does not promote overdependence or compromise a student's self-esteem.

Forming social relationships and fitting in are so important for many adolescents that they may show better impulse control and planning in the social arena than in the academic domain.

Jeana is a disorganized sixteen-year-old who was able to plan an amazing party when her parents were away. This does not mean that she has strong planning ability; rather, she was able to "rise to the occasion" to reach a specific short-term goal that was intrinsically motivating to her.

Teens that cannot keep up with the rapid fire rate of communication and have a hard time "reading between the lines" often face increasing social difficulties.

Rowan is a very bright fourteen-year-old who tends to blurt things out and interrupt others (due to a delay in the development of inhibition). Although he was popular in elementary school, he now has trouble keeping friends and doesn't understand why.

Young Adulthood:

During the late teens and early twenties, people continue to experience maturation of the frontal lobes with corresponding development of executive functioning. With experience and continued brain development come increased judgment, planning, and flexibility, all of which serve them well as they pursue further education, enter the workplace, or develop intimate relationships and assume family responsibilities.

Carlos is a nineteen-year-old who made a fairly smooth transition from high school to college. After missing a few too many

SPECIAL TRANSITION CONSIDERATIONS

For some young adults with executive delays, the transition from high school to college is a difficult one. Although a college education has great value, it is important to be creative and to keep an open mind when considering post-secondary options. Many different roads lead to independence and success in life. And sometimes the road winds quite a bit along the way.

For some students with executive weaknesses, a traditional college works well if the student has sufficient accommodations. For example, Olivia is a very bright eighteen-year-old who entered her freshman year with great hope and enthusiasm. However, she quickly became overwhelmed by the need to manage her time effectively and plan ahead. By mid-term exams, she was behind in her reading and was also having lots of trouble getting started on papers. By the end of the semester, no amount of cramming was sufficient to help her pass all of her courses, and she was placed on academic probation. With her parents' support, she decided to take a reduced course load and to work with an academic coach to help her build her executive skills. Her grades improved, and she began to feel more confident and hopeful again. She continues to take one less course each semester than the typical course load. She will graduate one year later than the students with whom she started.

For students with severe executive weaknesses who plan to attend college, it might work best to seek a school with a specific program for students with learning disabilities.

Sometimes, the common wisdom that a student should go to college immediately after high school graduation does not apply. Time off between high school and college may provide the opportunity for further maturation and for a student to develop the determination that comes with clearer goals.

Some people have strengths that lend themselves to careers for which college is not needed. Mentorships, apprentice positions, and other types of job opportunities that feature hands-on learning may work best for some.

8 a.m. classes as a college freshman, he figured out what he needed to do to successfully manage his courses while also enjoying a good amount of socializing. Now, in his sophomore year, he has begun applying for summer jobs and planning for his junior year abroad. Although Carlos enjoys age-appropriate executive skills, he still needs some financial, emotional, and practical support from his parents.

Some are late bloomers who may have difficulty in college or in their first work experiences but are then able to manage much better with continued maturation and experience. If your child fits into this category, you may need to provide more practical and emotional support for a longer time than you had planned or than was needed for your other children. Although some kids catch up, others need to develop ways of managing executive weaknesses as adults.

How Do I Know If My Child's Executive Skills Are Developing Normally?

Most parents know to seek help if their child is not walking by age two or talking by age three. But, when should a child be able to organize his notebook or keep track of his soccer clothes? Development varies widely and it is probably most useful to keep an eye on how peers are doing with these tasks. Teachers can also help you determine if your child seems to be on target with executive skills needed for school success.

Unlike "sitting up without support," "stringing two words together," or "recognizing primary colors," executive skills are never demonstrated in isolation; they overlap with motor, language, memory, and other cognitive skills. In their book entitled *Executive Skills in Children and Adolescents*, Drs. Peg Dawson and Richard Guare present a list of grade-typical developmental tasks requiring executive skills (see Table 3-1). This table provides an overview of behaviors that should be in place at various stages if your child is developing executive functions at a typical pace. If you have questions about whether your child's development is on target, you may find that a consultation with a professional, such as a psychologist or pediatrician, may be helpful. For more information regarding the evaluation process, refer to Chapter 6, Assessment: Figuring Out What's Wrong.

TABLE 3-1 Developmental Tasks Requiring Executive Skills

Age Range	Developmental Task
Preschool	• Run simple errands (e.g., "Get your shoes from the bedroom") • Tidy bedroom or playroom with assistance • Perform simple chores and self-help tasks with reminders (e.g., clear dishes from table, brush teeth, get dressed) • Inhibit behaviors: don't touch a hot stove; don't run into the street; don't grab a toy from another child; don't hit, bite, push, etc.
Kindergarten – Grade 2	• Run errands (two to three step directions) • Tidy bedroom or playroom • Perform simple chores, self-help tasks; may need reminders (e.g., make bed) • Bring papers to and from school • Complete homework assignments (20 minutes maximum) • Decide how to spend money (allowance) • Inhibit behaviors: follow safety rules, don't swear, raise hand before speaking in class, keep hands to self
Grades 3 - 5	• Run errands (may involve time delay or greater distance, such as going to a nearby store or remembering to do something after school) • Tidy bedroom or playroom (may include vacuuming, dusting, etc.) • Perform chores that take 15-30 minutes (e.g., clean up after dinner, rake leaves) • Bring books, papers, assignments to and from school • Keep track of belongings when away from home • Complete homework assignments (1 hour maximum) • Plan simple school projects such as book reports (select book, read book, write report) • Keep track of changing daily schedule (i.e., different activities after school) • Save money for desired objects; plan how to earn money • Inhibit/self-regulate: behave when teacher is out of the classroom; refrain from rude comments, temper tantrums, bad manners

Grades 6 – 8	• Help out with chores around the home, including both daily responsibilities and occasional tasks (e.g., emptying dishwasher, raking leaves, shoveling snow); tasks may take 60-90 minutes to complete • Baby-sit younger siblings or for pay • Use system for organizing schoolwork, including assignment book, notebooks, etc. • Follow complex school schedule involving changing teachers and changing schedules • Plan and carry out long-term projects, including tasks to be accomplished and reasonable timeline to follow; may require planning multiple large projects simultaneously • Plan time, including after school activities, homework, family responsibilities; estimate how long it takes to complete individual tasks and adjust schedule to fit • Inhibit rule breaking in the absence of visible authority
High School	• Manage schoolwork effectively on a day-to-day basis, including completing and handing in assignments on time, studying for tests, creating and following timelines for long-term projects, and making adjustments in effort and quality of work in response to feedback from teachers and others (e.g., grades on tests, papers) • Establish and refine a long-term goal and make plans for meeting that goal. If the goal beyond high school is college, the youngster selects appropriate courses and maintains grade point average (GPA) to ensure acceptance into college. The youngster also participates in extracurricular activities, signs up for and takes Scholastic Aptitude Tests (SATs) or American College Tests (ACTs) at the appropriate time, and carries out the college application process. If the youngster does not plan to go to college, he/she pursues vocational courses and, if applicable, employment outside of school to ensure the training and experience necessary to obtain employment after graduation • Make good use of leisure time, including obtaining employment or pursuing recreational activities during the summer • Inhibit reckless and dangerous behaviors (e.g., use of illegal substances, sexual acting out, shoplifting, or vandalism)

From Dawson, Peg & Richard Guare. *Executive Skills in Children and Adolescents: A Practical Guide to Assessment and Intervention,* Guilford Press, New York, N.Y., 2004. (Reprinted with permission.)

4

The Child's Experience of Executive Weaknesses

THE BASICS

> Efficient executive functioning is important for managing the practical demands of daily life.

> Executive weaknesses affect a child both in and out of school so the impact of weak executive functioning can be quite profound.

> Executive skills, such as impulse control and cognitive flexibility, also play a crucial role in managing social situations and dealing with stress.

> Some effects of executive weaknesses are *direct* in that the child or teen has trouble meeting expectations. Other effects are *indirect*, affecting a person's self-esteem and attitude.

> As parents, it is important to put ourselves in our child's place to understand her experience and to maintain a compassionate, helpful approach.

As frustrating and worrisome as it can be to raise a youngster with executive skill weaknesses, it is all the more frustrating for the child, herself. Whether a child expresses this frustration openly or presents an "I don't care" façade, her emotional development is intricately interwoven with her acquisition of executive skills. Sometimes, we need to step back and consider how these executive weaknesses affect the child's experience. How can we maintain a helpful, supportive approach without empathy for the child?

After all, executive skills must be considered in the context of a developing human being. At the same time that executive skills are progressing, kids are also developing emotionally and their experiences of themselves and their environment are coalescing into a self-image. The feedback that they get from the world around them, including from adults and peers, contributes positively or negatively to self-esteem and to the child's developing sense of herself.

Weak executive skills affect a youngster in many more ways than just how they perform in school, although this is often the impetus for seeking help. Kids receive feedback from people and from their environment in numerous ways over the course of a single day. So, let's look at a typical day and consider the child's experience of the daily routine. In the second half of the book, we offer suggestions for how you can help your child to meet these expectations. For now, though, let's focus on the child's experience.

Daily Life

Getting Started

The sun comes up and it's another new day! Full of hope and enthusiasm, you head into your daughter's room. Her alarm is beeping, but she is still lying in bed and has the covers pulled up to shut out the light and the sound. In your most cheerful voice you say, "Time to get up, Sweetheart. The bus will be here in forty-five minutes." That may be the last positive thing she hears from you that morning!

Think about what we ask of a child every morning: Get up on time, shift from sleep mode into action mode, keep track of time, complete a sequence of tasks that culminates in being dressed, fed, presentable, and ready to head out the door with all that she needs for the day.

Disorganized kids may become distracted or lose track of what they are supposed to be doing. Since many of them have problems keeping track of time, they only realize they are not ready at the very last minute (when they hear an irritated parent call out their name). Children with initiation difficulties need considerable help "getting going" and "keeping going." We have talked to many a parent who has discovered their child half-dressed and playing in her room when it is time to leave for school. We have also talked to many children who report that they just lose track of time. Often children promise to do better, because they feel badly about their lapses and really want to do what their parents are asking of them. Despite their promises, they have no clue how to change the situation.

Off to School

Schoolwork demands increasing levels of organization as the child goes from one grade to the next. Kids with executive weaknesses typically have more and more difficulty with each passing year. The most critical changes in school demands occur in mid-elementary school and at the transitions to middle and high school.

At all levels, though, adequate executive functions are generally taken for granted. Here are just some of the behaviors that we expect of children at school:

- pay attention to the teacher;
- remember and follow instructions;
- refrain from socializing with friends during class;
- interact with a range of peers during informal parts of the school day (during lunch, before and after school);
- remember your locker combination;
- bring the appropriate books and materials to class;
- work efficiently and rapidly on timed tasks;
- work slowly and carefully on more complex assignments; and
- move easily from room to room and subject to subject.

For students with executive weaknesses, a school day is filled with challenges to their performance and self-esteem. A child with weak working memory may struggle to follow directions while a child with weak self-monitoring skills may make "careless" mistakes and not tune into details. When a student has trouble with cognitive flexibility, changes or transitions throughout the school day may result in anxiety. These changes may be as common or seemingly benign as a substitute teacher, an assembly, or an assignment that is novel and unstructured. To an inflexible child, these can cause considerable discomfort or even meltdowns. Each of these experiences can result in negative feedback from school staff and personal concern as the child perceives a difference between her own performance and that of her peers.

After School

Finally, the students are let loose. Home again, the child now needs to face the after-school routine. Yes, that means homework.

Many students (and parents) have described homework time as the worst part of their day because of the level of tension within the family. Children may associate home with unstructured time and resist parental efforts to set routines around studying and homework completion. Worn out by the efforts of the day, students are ready to be free of demands. (Parents could use some down time, too!) The content of the homework may be frustrating if the work is difficult. Often, though, the homework itself takes relatively little time and effort (particularly in the early grades) compared to the time and energy it takes to gear-up to actually *do* the homework, which can be a struggle that is quite draining.

As students move along in school, homework and studying demands increase. As they get older, students understandably want more independence and may resist parental involvement in homework. At the same time, the students may actually need more supervision and support due to increasing work complexity and volume. In addition, some students who were able to do quite well on tests in earlier grades, simply by listening in class, have trouble adjusting to the need to more actively take notes, study, and prepare for tests in later grades.

Homework requires a child to:
- take down homework assignments and due dates;
- bring home the proper materials;
- properly estimate and budget the amount of time necessary to finish homework;
- break down an assignment into its component parts and do all the parts in sequence;
- work efficiently on simple assignments and work more carefully on more difficult projects;
- check work for errors and completeness;
- assemble all that is needed into the backpack; and
- remember to bring the assignments to class and turn the assignments in.

Is it any wonder that many children with executive weaknesses (and their parents) dread homework? Although executive function weaknesses are not an excuse for insufficient effort, we do understand why so many students engage in avoidance, procrastination, and even lying when it comes to homework.

Winding Down (The Evening Routine)

Just as important as the morning routine, the evening routine provides a structure that includes preparing for the next day and getting ready for bed. Some disorganized kids take a very long time to transition to bedtime. They may need reminders or physical supervision to brush their teeth, bathe/shower, pack for the next day, and settle into bed. We all know that it can be very helpful to select clothes, check the calendar, and pack lunches and backpacks the night before so that the morning routine runs more smoothly; however, to build these routines, many kids (even adolescents) need adult supervision and prompting.

Stressed and frustrated at the end of a long day, patience and understanding may be in short supply for both you and your child. Many kids who have "held it together" at school express their stress verbally or behaviorally at home. Without tolerating unacceptable or unsafe behavior, parents need to appreciate that children who must invest more effort than peers to meet demands and stay in control need to be able to vent frustration and "blow off steam." Many kids with poor self-monitoring have limited awareness of their fatigue and need help figuring out how best to manage stress. Note that some children and adolescents have good insight into the types of activities and routines that help them transition from the day to sleep.

Nighttime rituals and a slow progression towards bed and sleep help children to develop the sense of calm and soothing that allows them to give up the day with a feeling of well-being. Rituals construct a foundation of consistency and security that buffers against some of the challenges to your child's positive self-esteem. While younger kids may be comforted by listening to music, reading books, or snuggling with a parent before bed, adolescents should be supported in identifying how to "wind down" so that they get adequate rest before beginning the new day.

You and your child may have to give up some extracurricular activities to make the evening more relaxing. You may also have to start the routine much earlier than you would with another child to allow for your child's pace. However, both you and your child need some time to connect in a relaxed manner each evening. Depending upon temperament, some kids need a good amount of "alone time" while others crave interaction and personal contact.

Be mindful of your child's television-viewing habits if she has problems with sleep. Researchers have found that excessive television-viewing during the day and watching television before bedtime are associated with sleep disturbance. It appears that television-viewing overstimulates children, as opposed to granting them the sort of relaxation of being a "couch potato" that we tend to think it does. Research on this issue is not yet at the point of being able to definitively claim a direct cause-and-effect link between TV-viewing and sleep disturbance. However, the accumulation of data is clear in finding at least a correlation between television habits and sleep problems, including resistance to bedtime, delay in sleep onset, and anxiety around sleep. When children and adolescents have televisions in their bedrooms, problems with sleep are even more likely to occur. Our advice: If your child or adolescent does not have a television in her room, keep it that way. If she does, you might want to consider moving it out of the bedroom.

Chores

In addition to homework, kids are expected (we hope!) to help out around the house. This means that they need to follow through with daily expectations, track chores done only on specific days (e.g., taking out the trash), and do the job completely. For many children, chores are simply a part of the day, easily folded into the flow of the daily routine with only occasional reminders. However, chores can be a challenge for those with weak executive skills. Like homework time, chores can be seen as another demand by children who wish to be free of demands at the end of the school day.

We hear the same concerns about kids completing their chores around the house as we do about homework. Many parents we know have given up on requiring that their children do household chores in favor of putting all the emphasis on school-related work. Chores can be an important way to help kids build their executive skills in a non-academic setting. Just as important, there are great developmental benefits to learning to be a contributing member of the family group, with the self-esteem that follows from a sense of competence as additional payoff. The intervention chapters in the second half of this book will arm you with strategies for teaching your child to do homework *and* chores without all the nagging.

Friends and Social Life

Managing social situations is also challenging for many kids with weak executive control. The same impulsive responding, inflexibility, and poor self-monitoring that can get in the way of classroom performance can interfere with peer relationships. Just as academic demands increase as students progress through school, social situations also become more complex. For example, the kid who "doesn't know when to stop" may not be that different from the other kids, except that the other kids don't get caught because they are watching for the teacher and are paying good enough attention to others' reactions to stop shy of irritating.

Kids with weak impulse control are at significant risk for social difficulties due to interrupting, trouble with turn-taking, and insensitivity to others' feelings or reactions. Many impulsive children and adolescents desperately want to have friends and a social life but alienate

FACILITATING BETTER SOCIAL INTERACTIONS

Parents can help their children in the social realm by discreetly figuring out what is going wrong and helping to coordinate more successful social interactions. Jamal's mom sought a consultation with a psychologist because her son was becoming depressed, stating that nobody liked him. An energetic, "over the top" twelve-year-old, he felt sad at never being invited over to friends' houses and at being frequently ignored at school.

At the suggestion of the psychologist, Jamal's mom called the parents of one of his friends and learned that other kids enjoyed his sense of humor but became irritated because he always needed to control what they would do. With the cooperation of another parent, she invited a peer of Jamal's choosing to accompany their family on a tour of a "hands-on" science museum. Before the activity, Jamal's mom reminded Jamal that he would receive extra video game time for allowing his friend to decide which exhibits they visited and for thinking before acting. She told him that she would help by reminding him briefly if he started getting too bossy. With some verbal prompting and the help of a secret sign they had previously agreed upon, the outing was a success and Jamal began to consider that he could have more satisfactory peer interactions when he worked at controlling himself. Jamal and his mother made this a target behavior for a weekly reward and they continued to work on the goal of letting his friends choose activities. Later, they will need to work on building a collaborative approach to decision-making.

peers without understanding why kids don't want to spend time with them. It can be a painful process for kids who long to be included and accepted, and for their parents, too.

Children with cognitive rigidity may appear blunt, insensitive, and overly literal; they often have trouble reading social cues. They tend to rely heavily on rules and have trouble determining when the situation requires a more diplomatic response. When children are quite young, it is the parents' job to teach the basic rules. "Always tell the truth." "Never break the rules." However, as kids get older, they begin to understand the shades of gray, and that rules are not absolute. Fortunately, most typically developing kids figure out that there are exceptions to all rules. However, children with cognitive rigidity have trouble with the exceptions to the rules. For example, a general rule may be, "Use an inside voice. Don't scream." Although this is usually the case, it may be appropriate to scream at a basketball game or if someone is in danger. Since it is impossible to actually teach a child all of the possible exceptions to rules of conduct, cognitively inflexible kids may be quite confused by these situations.

Characterized by "black-or-white" thinking, kids with this profile tend to adhere rigidly to rules and expect others to do the same. When a middle school student points her finger at a peer and says, "Bus driver, she is chewing gum and that is not allowed," there are liable to be social consequences that she has not anticipated. That child, who is just trying to do what she thinks is right, may earn the reputation of a tattletale. Her compulsion to strictly adhere to rules makes her easily misunderstood, leading to unfair treatment from her peers. In more severe cases, she may wind up a victim of teasing, bullying, and other social cruelty.

In addition to ensuring that vulnerable children and adolescents have adequate supervision, parents, teachers, and other important adults can help inflexible kids develop increased social competence and coping skills that may buffer them from secondary emotional distress. We discuss some of these approaches in Chapter 12: Helping Children Shift Gears.

Emotions

As we noted above, executive skills do not develop in a vacuum. We need to remember that a child's temperament, or personality, also plays a big role in her attitude, perceptions, and responses to executive weaknesses.

Temperament

You probably already appreciate that your child came into the world with some characteristics and features that are not in any way related to experience. A child's temperament encompasses some very clear preferences and characteristics. This is particularly apparent if you have more than one child.

Take sisters, Carol and Kayla. Carol has always had a "glass half full" perspective. When she spills her juice, she pops up, gets a paper towel, tells her dad, "Don't worry, I'll take care of it," cleans up the spill, and quickly returns to what she was doing. When Kayla spills her juice, on the other hand, she automatically apologizes multiple times, begins to worry that her parents will evaluate her negatively, and can't stop thinking about her mistake. Her "hard-wiring" results in a more pessimistic view of herself and the world.

How you respond to your child, as well as how your child responds to you and to life experiences, is interactive. For those who seek to please adults, meet expectations, and perform well, there is rarely the need to question motivation. It is clear that Kayla, from our example above, cares about how she is doing, as she is the first one to call attention to her shortcomings and to vow to work harder when she experiences failure or inconsistency. However, many children and adolescents with executive dysfunction or delays react to frustration and failure with decreased effort, avoidance, and declarations that they "don't care." Although both groups of kids are at risk for social, emotional, and daily living difficulties, those who deny their difficulties and who adopt an "I could not care less" attitude pose notable challenges for their parents and teachers. We encourage these important adults to look beyond the surface presentation to see the underlying weaknesses and frustration.

Self-Understanding and Self-Esteem

One of our most important jobs as parents is to help our kids develop a realistically positive self-image. Good self-esteem is built on a levelheaded appraisal of one's own strengths and weaknesses and a sense of competence in the world. People who view themselves as helpless, ineffective, or inferior are at risk for lifelong problems in social, emotional, and vocational functioning. On the other hand, people who deny their own weaknesses and fail to realistically appraise themselves will have an inflated view of their abilities and will be unprepared for the real world.

Given the fact that children and adolescents with executive weaknesses may experience more disappointment and frustration than their peers, there is a notable risk of developing negative self-esteem. We have talked with many kids who have come to believe that they are just not smart enough or not trying hard enough. Like many of their parents and teachers, they are frustrated by the fact that they can sometimes excel but often fall short of expectations. How do we help children to feel good about themselves in the face of their weaknesses?

In addition to acknowledging and encouraging kids in their areas of strength, it is important that we help them to understand their own weaknesses and put them into context. Even in the most supportive of environments, negative feedback arises from the fact that a person with executive weaknesses is out of synch with expectations. Such experiences play a powerful role in self-assessment. You cannot (and should not!) convince a child that everything is fine when that child's experiences confirm a weakness. What parents can do is to help the child to express her feelings about the experiences, develop a straightforward approach to the problems, and work on problem-solving. In our examples in the second half of the book, these principles are in action. Although it is important to help kids understand their weaknesses, it is also important to convey that these alone do not define them as a person.

In addition to parents' input on these issues, professionals can play a strong role in the process. It can start with the initial evaluation/assessment and an explanation of the results with the child geared to her level of understanding and emotional development. (For more information on the assessment process, refer to Chapter 6.) Sometimes, parents worry about how we will summarize evaluation results when we meet with their kids. They express concerns about the possible negative effects to self-esteem and they worry that talking about problems will make the child feel different from peers. In reality, many kids view their problems and differences as more severe than they actually are. They also often underestimate their true strengths. Our goal is to help kids understand their difficulties without defining themselves by them or becoming overwhelmed. We don't like to hear someone say "I am AD/HD." In fact, although she may have attentional weaknesses, she is so much more than the sum of these and it does her a disservice to focus exclusively on these characteristics. On the other hand, research clearly indicates that students with disabilities are most successful in college when they are able to clearly and comfortably discuss their strengths and needs as good self-advocates. Working toward this level of self-understanding and confidence requires beginning much earlier, by supporting honest self-appraisal and acknowledgement of strengths and weaknesses. As parents, you have the power to play the biggest role in this process.

5

Impact on the Family

➤ Living with a child who has executive weaknesses affects the whole family.

➤ The complexity of setting realistic expectations for a disorganized, impulsive child typically causes parental stress and may lead to burnout. For some families, this is a source of chronic stress.

➤ Parents sometimes feel isolated from family and friends who do not understand the nature of their struggles.

➤ Siblings may feel irritated, resentful, or forgotten in response to the level of parental attention and energy directed at their disorganized brother or sister.

➤ Some parents experience executive function weaknesses, themselves, which makes it even more challenging to provide the external consistency and support that their kids need.

All parents experience times of frustration and fatigue. The physical demands of the job and the emotional strain of meeting others' needs is an ongoing source of stress.

Another stressful facet of the task is the angst of uncertainty and worry. Am I doing what is right for my child? Will my child turn out okay? If parents had a crystal ball that showed them that their children would, in time, grow into happy and productive adults, then they could relax. Of course, there is no such way to see into the future, and the worry contributes to a sort of undercurrent that adds to the routine stress of parenting.

However, for parents of children who have developmental delays or disabilities, the worries are even larger. Their strain is magnified by the fact that their children are out of synch with their peers and with the demands of the world. Will they ever find their niche? Will they ever learn to compensate well enough to manage the demands of life? Will they find partners who will love and accept them? Can they succeed at a job and support themselves? Parents of children with disabilities also have the added demands of providing extra supervision, monitoring, and direct help for a longer period of time than is required for their peers and siblings.

Dr. Russell Barkley, an international expert on AD/HD, recommends that parents of children with AD/HD think about their children as having a *true* disability. Since your child's weaknesses are essentially invisible, we're not always as charitable about dealing with his ongoing problems as we might be if he had a physical handicap. Maintaining a "disability perspective" means that we keep in mind that the child has a weakness that is no less real for being less overt.

In the same way, it may help to think of your job as the parent of a young child or adolescent with executive weaknesses as a source of chronic stress. This does not mean that the job is not satisfying or that you never have wonderful, surprising, joyful moments with your child. It *does* mean that you are at higher risk for burnout, and you should be aware of some of the common pitfalls among families of kids with disabilities.

Impact on Parents

Your level of stress depends on a variety of factors, including the severity of your child's difficulties, your own temperament, and your network of support. The severity and nature of your child's difficulties may affect such important things as whether you are able to take your child along for routine outings or special events. Is your child difficult to handle in public places? Does your child have difficulty getting along with peers? Does your teenager ask questions that embarrass peers and adults? Is your adolescent able to competently care for his younger siblings? These variables affect how easily you can go about your life and how much stress you experience.

Your own temperament affects how you handle and how you interpret the demands of your job as a parent, as well. Are you a person who easily takes charge of situations? Someone who can think clearly in the midst of chaos? Or do you get overwhelmed by the action swirling around you? Do you, yourself, struggle with executive weaknesses? Do you tend to get bogged down by worries about what others think? Or can you act based on your own knowledge of your child without taking the looks or comments of others too much to heart?

The more informed you are about your child's needs, and the more comfortable you are with your own expertise, the less prone to burnout you will be. So, educating yourself is a healthy move. Learn what you can about your child and about executive weaknesses, in general. If you are having trouble staying on an even keel, consider a consultation with a mental health professional to air your concerns and get back on track.

Adding to the stress of parenting a child with executive weaknesses is the isolation that can occur. Parents often feel that their friends and relatives just do not understand their situation. The symptoms of executive skills problems are generic enough that it is sometimes hard for people to see them as other than just bad behavior or signs of poor parenting. Parents of kids with poor executive functioning often hear:

"Memory problems? I think he just remembers what he wants to remember."

"Joey is just manipulating you. What do you mean he can't organize his room on his own?"

"You are enabling him. How do you expect him to learn to be more responsible if you keep helping him?"

We have found over the years that sometimes the "helicopter parent" who is accused of hovering is, in fact, providing the appropriate level of support for the child. Of course, some parents really do need a bit of a push to move out of the "protector" role. If you have questions about the level of support your child needs, we hope that this book helps you answer some of those questions. If you are still unsure, even after your efforts to educate yourself, then consultation with a professional with specific expertise in executive skills development can help. Local chapters of organizations that advocate for children with disabilities are a good source of referrals to qualified professionals. Other parents, as well as professionals who work with children and adolescents, are also good resources.

You should also be aware that individuals who feel part of a larger community tend to experience less stress. Do you have a strong circle of friends? Is your extended family a source of support? Are you grounded by a church, synagogue, or other religious community? Do you belong to other groups or organizations? All of these provide a buffer against feelings of isolation.

You may need to push yourself to stay connected with others, particularly when you are feeling weary and stretched thin from the demands of daily life. If you are having difficulty finding other parents who understand your concerns, look for local chapters of organizations or online forums designed to educate and advocate for children with specific disabilities. These can be a great resource for information and support.

Impact on Siblings

By definition, having a sibling means that your parents' time, effort, and energy are divided among you and your sisters or brothers. That is both the beauty and the challenge of learning to live with siblings. Each of the children learns that his needs do not always come first. Over time, children learn that the good of the family or of a specific family member sometimes trumps their own needs or wishes.

"It's not fair!" is the universal battle cry of siblings. Typical sibling conflicts can be magnified by the fact a child with special needs requires more support and guidance than do the child's siblings. Brothers and sisters of disorganized kids are likely resent the sib with special needs, and are also worried and confused about their sibling's difficulties. Siblings are likely to feel jealous of the amount of attention directed to the child with special needs.

Educating kids about their brother's or sister's weaknesses (and his or her strengths!) helps to create a supportive family. Sometimes, siblings can be big supporters of the child with special needs. Do not expect this to cure sibling rivalry which, at its best, is a healthy and normal striving to capture parents' attention. What you are looking for is a balance of feelings, so that your children's irritation with each other is punctuated with moments of connection and genuine concern.

Setting aside separate time for each child goes a long way toward meeting each child's need to feel appreciated. During this time, focus on your special bond with that one child. Create a ritual for the two of you, such as Monday evenings with Mom or Saturday breakfast at the local diner with Dad. Enlist a family member or sitter to stay with the other children every now and then, and have a play date with only one child. It will do you both good!

And of course, you need to keep the golden rule of raising siblings in mind. That is, fair does not mean equal or the same treatment for all. Being fair means offering to each child what she or he needs.

Impact on Couples

Raising a child with a disability takes a toll on couples, too. There may be conflict directly related to the parent role, as well as fallout from the stress. It is not unusual for couples to disagree about how to interpret a disorganized, impulsive child's behavior. Most of us rely on our own experiences growing up to help us determine expectations and what our children should be able to do independently. If one or both parents were strong, naturally-organized students, it is likely to be difficult to understand a disorganized child. We often meet with parents who each have very different explanations for their child's underachievement and inconsistent performance. One parent may view the child as not trying hard enough while his partner or spouse may see the child's difficulties as related to developmental or brain-based weaknesses. One parent may feel that the other needs to be more understanding. The other parent may feel that more strict discipline is the answer.

When parents disagree about something as basic as how to raise a child, the resulting underlying tension is sure to affect the whole family. Give these issues the attention they deserve. Each of you needs to be educated about your child's difficulties and you need to find time to consider together what your approach will be. If you cannot come to a shared agreement, seek outside input from a professional who works with parents and knows the ins and outs of daily life with a youngster who has developmental weaknesses. If your disagreements are more pervasive than just child-related concerns, seek out someone whose focus is on helping couples develop better communication and conflict resolution skills.

Even when parents are generally in agreement about expectations and their child's needs, parenting a child with special needs can be a significant source of stress in the relationship. While most of us look forward to having more time alone and as a couple as our kids get older, many of these children continue to require considerable parent time and supervision.

Take care of your relationship with your partner. Carve out some time for just the two of you to go out and do something you enjoy. It will make you a better and happier parent in the long run.

Special Situations

When the Apple Does Not Fall Far From the Tree

Imagine the following: You are sitting in one of our offices as we describe your child's strengths, and then we explain that the reason he is having such difficulty is because of executive function weaknesses. When we get to the part about recommendations and what he needs to be successful, you keep hearing an emphasis on the need for adult-provided structure and support for a longer period of time than is typical. But what if you share your child's weaknesses? Perhaps organization and timeliness are not your strong suits. What if you have trouble with planning and sticking to a structure yourself? Panic may be your first response! Feelings of guilt and self-blame may follow.

Perhaps we can help you to take a different approach to your experience, because there is a silver lining to your cloud. Remember that your child has the advantage of being raised by a parent who truly understands his difficulties, a companion on the journey of learning better skills for self-management. If you have first-hand experience with executive weaknesses, you may be able to understand your child's difficulties in a way that others cannot.

However, if you have executive weaknesses yourself, you likely need help to create the consistency, predictability, and order that your child needs. Enlist the aid of family members and other adults in your child's life. Although parents may be the obvious choice to provide the support that a child needs, other folks, including teachers, coaches, tutors, friends, and extended family members, can serve the same role. Seek professional resources for yourself if you need help with developing strategies for managing tasks.

Single Parents

Being a single parent presents a range of challenges. Having sole responsibility for raising a child who needs a high level of support and supervision can be tricky and exhausting. For single parents, identifying other adults who can provide daily support is essential. Even the most patient, understanding parent needs some respite from the constant demands of caring for a child. Maintaining a strong network of support from family, friends, and the community becomes all the more critical when you are a single parent. Seek others with whom you can share your joys and worries about your child.

Divorced or Separated Parents Who Share Custody

Although it can certainly be done effectively, co-parenting a child after a divorce or separation can be challenging. Disorganized kids may have trouble transitioning between homes and may need considerable help planning which possessions they need to move between households. To the extent that you offer a common, consistent structure and daily routine at both houses, your child can more easily negotiate the transitions.

In addition, many students with executive weaknesses require close communication between school and home. This may mean that teachers and other school staff need to remain in contact with two sets of parents. You need to sit down together with the school staff at the beginning of each school year to determine the best way to accomplish this.

Disorganized kids and their separated parents also face the challenge of keeping track of sports schedules and social engagements. When possible, duplicate sets of cleats, textbooks, clothes, and other possessions can help. Still, planning and coordination can be a daunting task. Of course, communication and cooperation are always the goal in co-parenting arrangements.

Staying Healthy

Self-care is the cornerstone of any plan designed to help you manage the stress of parenting a youngster with executive weaknesses. Consider building into your life healthy ways to regulate your stress level. Regular exercise, yoga classes, and meditation are just a few of the ways to stay centered. All the things that promote your general physical health, including good nutrition and adequate sleep, also keep your mind on an even keel and improve your outlook.

To do what is best for your child, you must make it a priority to attend to your own self-care. Remember what they tell you on an airplane: If the oxygen level drops, those who are caring for others should put the oxygen mask over their own faces first.

6

Assessment: Figuring Out What's Wrong

THE BASICS

➢ Assessment serves a variety of functions:
  - rules out "look-alike" conditions;
  - determines which executive skills are problematic;
  - defines the severity of the problem;
  - identifies co-occurring disorders; and
  - helps parents and teachers understand the whole child—strengths as well as weaknesses.

➢ It can be very confusing to navigate the many types of testing that are completed by many different professionals.

➢ Assessing executive functions can be challenging. It is important for the examiner to look at multiple sources of information, including performance on formal tests as well as how the child functions in daily life.

One of the first steps in the process of helping a child with executive weaknesses is to figure out exactly what is going wrong. We need to generate an individualized profile of strengths and weaknesses in order to be able to develop specific plans that help the child and to take into account the child's areas of strength.

The Purpose of Assessment

The characteristics of executive dysfunction are generic, meaning that they are not specific to only one condition or disorder. Problems can occur for many reasons. To illustrate, consider a child with a skin rash. A doctor needs to see what the rash looks like, learn about any other symptoms, and be familiar with the patient's health history before designing a treatment plan. Just as your child's doctor first must understand the nature of the rash to treat it correctly, problems with executive skills require a thorough assessment in order to understand and treat. Remember that there is no blood test or biological marker that pinpoints these conditions. Instead, we have to look at how the child is functioning and then use this information to make inferences about the underlying nature of the problem.

When done well, these evaluations can be quite time-consuming and expensive if done by a private professional. So, why do we need them?

1. The assessment process is important to "rule in" executive weaknesses and "rule out" look-alike conditions.

The first task in assessment is to make sure that we understand the nature of the problem. Are the problems truly consistent with a diagnosis of "executive dysfunction?" If so, we need to look at all the possible reasons a person could have these problems so we can rule out look-alike conditions. A child can be disorganized, have trouble initiating tasks, or have difficulty with any of the other executive skills for many different reasons.

Some of the possible look-alike conditions are social-emotional difficulties, weaknesses in language, or other learning disabilities. For example, some kids who have trouble processing language appear inattentive. When they cannot understand or remember incoming information, they lose focus and "look" similar to children with AD/HD. Similarly, a youngster with a math learning disability may have trouble concentrating when completing math work and may rush to get the work done as quickly as possible. An evaluation will help to determine whether her tendency to work too quickly is observed on other tasks, as well, or whether it appears to be secondary to her math disorder. Finally, a child who is anxious or depressed often has trouble with concentration, which could easily be mistaken for a primary problem with attention if the assessment doesn't look at current emotional functioning and stress levels.

If we do not understand the role of information-processing, learning disabilities, or emotional issues, our intervention recommendations may not be effective. A thorough assessment screens for these using a combination of interviews with primary caretakers, questionnaires filled out by caretakers and teachers, interview and observation of the child, and functional tests. "Functional tests" mean simply that we test how a child is doing in that area. These in-office tests are conducted one-on-one and involve asking questions, requiring the child to complete "hands-on" tasks, or to work independently. Whether testing is done by the school or a private professional, it should take place in a separate room which is relatively free of distractions.

2. The assessment process is important to determine which executive skills are problematic and to understand their impact on daily life.

The second purpose of an assessment is to understand the child's particular profile of executive strengths and weaknesses. As we outlined earlier, there are many different, but related, executive skills and it is rare for one, alone, to be out of whack.

Understanding a child's specific profile is much more helpful than saying generally that she has trouble with executive functioning. For example, what we do to help a child with working memory weaknesses may be very different from what we put into place for someone who has trouble getting started with work.

Often, for example, parents come to us stating, "I already know that my child has AD/HD, so I don't need any testing." Now, while people with AD/HD make up a very large percentage of those with executive dysfunction, simply knowing that someone does or does not have AD/HD is not enough information for developing a treatment plan. Unless the child has recently been evaluated and the report provides the data we need, at least a partial evaluation is required for good planning. A partial evaluation might involve interviews with the parents and the child, and collecting observational data from parents and teachers via structured rating scales.

A comprehensive evaluation outlines the profile of executive strengths and weaknesses both by gathering information about what others have observed regarding the child's executive functioning and by observing the child's behavior directly through testing. How does the child do on very structured tasks (such as simple questions) versus those with less of an inherent structure (such as those requiring longer responses or involving open-ended questions)? How does the child perform on tasks that require her to remember bits of information? On timed tasks, does the child get right down to work or does she seem unaware of the need to perform in a timely fashion? Importantly, the information is not always in the test scores, themselves. Sometimes the information comes from the observations of a skilled and experienced examiner. How a child approaches a task is as important as how well she performs overall. Although some children and adolescents lack awareness of their weaknesses, it is also important to talk with kids about their own experiences and perceptions.

If we find evidence of problems in the development of executive skills, then we also try to get a good picture of how the child is actually doing in her daily life to determine the extent and pervasiveness of the problem. This is where reviewing the history, interviews with those who know the child, and structured questionnaires about executive skills can be very useful.

3. The assessment process is important to put the profile of executive skills into the context of the whole child.

As we mentioned in a previous chapter, knowing about a child's executive skills does not mean that we understand the whole person. We need to place this understanding into the context of a larger profile of strengths and weaknesses. This serves two purposes. First, we need to know if there are other areas of development that require intervention. It is very common to have what are called "co-morbid disorders." This simply means that there are other significant problems that occur along with the executive skills deficits. If we treat only one part of the problem, the child will not achieve the success we are hoping for.

For example, many kids with AD/HD (who always have executive weaknesses) also have learning disabilities and other developmental disorders. In one of the best studies of AD/HD to date (Multimodal Treatment Study of Children with ADHD), 70 percent of the children with AD/HD also met criteria for another behavioral or emotional disorder.

People are complicated and a variety of factors may contribute to a child's disorganization, e.g., cognitive (executive) delays, emotional difficulties, and a lack of structure or organization in the environment. By doing a thorough assessment, we can understand the factors in play and then plan and implement effective interventions. The professional who evaluates your child can also help you prioritize which interventions to try first.

TIP: Although we know that kids can benefit from different types of services and programs, we need to balance the need for intervention with having adequate time for play, relaxation, rest, family, and friends.

Putting it all together, let's take eleven-year-old Kent as an example. His parents pursued an evaluation because of his increased frustration and declining grades. The assessment indicated ADD (AD/HD, Predominantly Inattentive Type) with significant weaknesses in initiation, planning, organization, and self-monitoring, as well as notable anxiety. In addition to recommending that Kent's parents request a range of supports and accommodations at school, medical consultation for AD/HD and anxiety was also recommended. Further, the evaluator recommended that the family work with a mental health provider to serve as a sort of case manager and also to teach their son skills for coping with his anxious feelings. The examiner referred the family to professionals with expertise in treating kids with both AD/HD and anxiety.

In addition to understanding and planning treatment for co-morbidities, a thorough evaluation helps parents understand children by profiling strengths as well as weaknesses. Knowing a child's strengths lets us help the child build on those competencies and provides information about the kinds of things that motivate the child. All of this information is critical to knowing and planning for an individual.

Evaluating the Role of Expectations

In some cases, we have seen children without executive weaknesses who are struggling because school or the demands in other setting are just too high for their typically-developing abilities. Sometimes, the expectations built into the curriculum are advanced, relative to the average child's abilities. This is the case for some very selective schools as well as for some high-achieving public schools. Perhaps a school change is indicated.

Sometimes, too, a child with only mild executive weaknesses experiences big problems because the adults in her life are themselves so disorganized. Again, this is where a thorough evaluation that looks at all the possible contributing factors can help to pinpoint other necessary interventions. Perhaps the whole family needs help with developing organizational strategies that work. These are things that should be considered by an evaluator.

You can always do a consultation with a professional to help you figure out if a full evaluation is even needed. In some cases you may already have a good enough understanding of the issues to move directly to intervention.

Who Does Testing and What Do They Test?

Neuropsychological testing? Psychoeducational evaluation? Psychological assessment? Help! What do these all mean, how are they different, and what professionals are qualified to give me the answers I need?

Let's keep it simple. Regardless of who signs the report and what the evaluation is called, you need someone who is qualified to address the following broad areas of development:

- Cognitive ability ("I.Q.")
- Language-based skills
- Visually-based skills
- Visual-motor integration
- Memory
- Attention
- Executive functions
- Academic achievement
- Social-emotional factors

A variety of professionals perform testing, including psychologists (school psychologists, clinical psychologists, and neuropsychologists), educational specialists, speech/language pathologists (SLP), occupational therapists (OT), and physical therapists (PT). Additionally, physicians (pediatricians, family practitioners, psychiatrists, and neurologists) contribute valuable information to the diagnostic process. Depending on the specific problem areas your child presents, one or more evaluators from different disciplines may be needed to get a full picture of your child.

Let us be clear about our bias: We are psychologists and we feel that well-trained psychologists who specialize in evaluation and child development are generally a good place to start in your efforts to help your child. An experienced psychologist may serve as a sort of case manager, coordinating the diagnostic team.

Should You Seek Assessment through the Public School System or from a Private Professional?

You have the right to request testing for your child from your local public school, even if your child attends a private school. Federal laws that govern testing, special education services, and accommodations for students include Section 504 of the Rehabilitation Act and the Individuals with Disabilities Education Act (IDEA 2004). Since these are complex pieces of legislation, we list further resources at the end of the book. In addition to educating yourself about the law, you may want to obtain information from a parent advocacy organization that focuses on your child's disabilities. Some families choose to hire a consultant who specializes in understanding individual learning profiles and collaborating with schools, such as a psychologist or private educational advocate.

We cannot tell you whether evaluation through the public school system or a private professional is best for your child; however here are some factors you should consider before making your decision:

- *Cost*—All public education is funded by your taxes. That means that you have already paid for services through the public schools. An evaluation through the school requires no additional cost. On the other hand, a private professional charges you for her time and expertise. Although customary fees vary too widely for us to give specifics, it is a significant expense. Sometimes, medical insurance covers a portion of the evaluation fee, particularly for the neuropsychological and emotional (psychological) testing, if that is needed. Most insurance companies expect that testing for learning disabilities and other academic concerns will be covered by schools and describe testing in those areas as "not medically necessary." If you are wondering if any of the testing may be reimbursed by your insurance company, make sure you obtain that information before any testing occurs.

- *Scope of the evaluation*—In accordance with federal mandates, evaluations completed by schools focus on educating a student up to the level of her peers rather than optimizing development. Further, the school's focus is on factors affecting performance in the classroom and may not include evaluation and recommendations to help the child outside of school.

Parents who pursue evaluation through their public school are a part of the team that determines if testing is required, and if so, what testing will be done. However, in some instances, parents may disagree with the rest of the team's decision on what to test, or on the results of the entire evaluation. Subsequently, parents may seek consultation from a private professional about whether to appeal a decision with which they disagree.

Parents may choose to work with a private professional in conjunction with the public school team or independent of it. Private professionals typically pursue a complete profile, without limiting assessment to the single arena of education. The resulting profile identifies a student's strengths and makes recommendations for propelling the child toward her full potential both in school and outside of school.

- *Time*—Federal guidelines define how long the school system has to complete each step of the process from your initial written request to completing the testing and presenting the results. These dictate the maximum amount of time that the school system may take, but the actual amount of time may be less. Be sure to ask your school team how long they anticipate it will take to get through the process and to apprise you of what the law states about timelines and your rights.

  If you would like the final assessment to include testing results from a private professional, make sure you coordinate schedules. Timelines vary widely from one private professional to another, so it is important to be clear on the time frame with regard to completing testing and receiving the final report when you contract for testing from a private professional.

  If you are submitting a private evaluation report to your child's school team, find out how much time they need to review it before you can meet to discuss the report and the school's plan for meeting your child's needs.

- *Confidentiality*—When testing is done by the school system, the test results become a part of your child's permanent record and are communicated to members of the school team. The results travel with your child's file to each public school. Safeguards are built into the system regarding how the information is stored, who has access to the file, and preventing release outside the school system without the permission of the parent or guardian.

When testing is done privately, the parent or guardian owns the information. Except in unusual legal situations, the report goes only to you unless you sign a consent form authorizing release of the information to other specifically identified individuals.

We understand that the decision to go with a public school-based evaluation or a private assessment is an important one. We have already shared our bias that obtaining more comprehensive information is often the best way to plan interventions. Parents have more direct control over the private testing process. However, some public schools do a very good job and may be able to relatively quickly complete a range of multidisciplinary evaluations (e.g., psychoeducational, speech and language, and occupational therapy). Further, some families may simply be unable to afford the cost of a private evaluation. Whichever route you choose, you need to be an active participant in the process. Read the section below for important information about how to be an educated consumer so that you can effectively advocate for your child.

How to Be an Educated Consumer

So, how do you find a qualified professional to evaluate your child and produce an independent educational evaluation (IEE)? One of your best sources of information is other parents who have been through the testing process. You may also want to talk with professionals such as teachers, pediatricians, and others who work with children and adolescents. Local, regional, and national organizations that advocate for children with disabilities may also be able to direct you to qualified professionals. If possible, talk with a few examiners to get a feel for their approach and an idea about the best personality "fit" with your child. In most cases, it is important to make sure that the professional understands educational law and school procedures so that any privately conducted testing covers the information that the school team needs in order to move forward with interventions. Ask about the person's education, training, and experience. Even if an evaluator has impressive credentials, you need to make sure that she will take the time necessary to listen to you and get to know your child.

If your child has difficulty feeling comfortable with new people or is anxious or sensitive, check to see if she can do a quick visit to the office before her first testing session. Particularly for younger children, arrange to have snacks and prizes available if they will help pave the way for a positive testing experience. Unlike spelling and other school tests, children are not to be prepared for testing except to get a good night sleep the night before and encouraged to do their best. (If you have the testing done at your child's school, you cannot select the evaluator but can request notification of when the testing will occur so that you can support your child.)

Once you have selected a professional to complete the assessment, make sure you clearly understand her business practices (e.g., fees, policy for missed appointments, insurance participation, type of payment accepted, etc.) and when to expect the results. It is important to agree upon the questions to be answered and the scope of the evaluation. Before the first session, the evaluator should help you find a good way of explaining the testing process to your child, as it is important for her to feel comfortable and to understand how testing (and the time and effort we are asking her to invest) will be helpful. Gaining trust and "buy-in" is particularly important for adolescents who may be wary of any attempts to figure out what is "wrong" with them.

If you are requesting testing from your child's public school, be sure you make a formal request in writing and address it to the designated "IEP chairperson." (Call the school office to find out who this is in your child's school.) Keep a copy of the letter for your personal home files. The school will follow up by inviting you to a meeting, often called a "screening" or "child study meeting," to consider your request. At that meeting, you will also be given the school district's written guide to your rights and procedural safeguards so you will understand how to appeal the team's decision if you disagree.

If you decide to have testing done by your child's school, you may want to hire a psychologist or other professional to review the results and give an independent opinion about the conclusions and recommendations. Although there is a downside to doing the evaluation in pieces, it sometimes makes sense to pursue testing through the public school and then have additional testing completed privately, if needed.

We want to emphasize the importance of taking an active role in the assessment process. Ask questions at every step! If you don't understand the answer, ask again! Ask the professionals to use real-life language and to give examples if they are using jargon that is foreign to you. Be sure you understand the scope of the testing, what questions the evaluation is designed to answer, and what the test results mean.

If you are left with nagging doubts about what it all means or if there is more that can be done, then it is time to seek a second opinion. Private professionals who specialize in this arena (see below for how to find a qualified professional) are frequently called upon to review evaluations completed by schools or by other professionals and to help families understand their implications. Remember that the test scores alone are rarely sufficient to help us understand a child's strengths and needs. Sometimes, the scores do not help us figure out the 'whys': Why a bright student keeps forgetting to turn in completed homework; Why there is so much variability between math test scores; or, Why a previously successful student has come to hate school. Many students with executive weaknesses do fine on in-office and classroom tests but have true problems with learning and performance.

The Evaluation Process

Evaluations generally start with an initial information-gathering process. Sometimes the problems are so clear and specific that the initial data collection process directs the interventions, and no further testing is required. In most cases, however, collecting relevant information is just the beginning of the evaluation. If this is the first evaluation of your child or if you are asking the school for help, it is particularly important that the assessment be comprehensive enough to fully delineate the strengths and weaknesses in your child's cognitive profile. If your child is struggling after an evaluation and strategies that were put into place to help the child aren't working, it is important to find out why through another evaluation.

A comprehensive evaluation usually includes:

- Review of medical, developmental, and school history
- Analysis of school records
- Parent and teacher ratings of the child's behavior completed via questionnaires; older children and adolescents also complete rating scales
- Interviews with the parents, teachers, child, and other professionals (e.g., tutor, counselor, physician), some of which may be conducted by phone

- School observation, if indicated
- Test administration

The total amount of time, length of each session, and specific tests vary. The evaluation is designed to find out why your child is struggling, and depending on the complexity and what the evaluator learns along the way, more testing may be needed. Additionally, children work at different rates, so it is not possible to predict exactly how long it takes for an individual child to complete the tests. The evaluator who does the scheduling takes into account your child's age, attention span, and stamina. Some evaluators conduct testing for a full day while others break testing into smaller sessions. Some of the tests are timed, while others are untimed. The evaluator can work to make sure your child is comfortable but cannot change the standardized instructions and procedures. Understand that the evaluator is supportive of your child's needs but also makes demands of your child by asking your child to perform. This is the nature of testing.

The evaluator selects appropriate tests that cover the developmental skills in question. Tests are revised and updated regularly, and new tests are published based on theoretical and research advances. Please see Appendix A for a list of some of the most commonly used measures of executive functioning.

Here's our dirty little secret about executive function assessment. Testing is done one-on-one, generally in an environment with minimal distractions, and by an evaluator who provides a certain level of structure. Sometimes, this format compensates for executive skill weaknesses in such a way that the child looks more competent during the testing sessions than in real life. So, it is possible to have adequate scores on formal measures of executive functions and *still* have real-life performance and executive problems. This is where the clinical experience of the examiner and integration of relevant information about day-to-day functioning are essential.

Once the Assessment is Done

Following the formal assessment process, parents are invited to discuss results of the evaluation and specific recommendations tailored to the child's unique profile. This typically happens a few weeks after testing is completed with a full written report to follow. In many instances, it is helpful for the examiner to have a brief discussion of the test results with the child, in a way the child can understand. For some kids, the parent is present; for others, it makes more sense for the examiner to talk to the child or teen alone. That review should emphasize the child's strengths as well as discuss ways of addressing weaknesses.

When testing has been done privately, the report is only provided to the school with written parental permission. An exception is when the school has agreed to fund an independent educational evaluation (IEE) or when a special education hearing officer has ordered one; in those cases, the report will be provided to both the parents and the school.

If parents obtain a private evaluation and choose not to submit the report to the school, the school may request to perform their own testing so that they can determine whether or not your child needs individualized services or a change to the existing plan, if there is one already in place. In this case, you should provide a list of tests and procedures completed as part of the private evaluation, since many tests cannot be readministered within one year's time.

Most likely, you will want to share the assessment results with your child's school. The school team is generally pleased to have more information to use to determine how to proceed. However, be advised that while the school team must *consider* the evaluation, they do not

WHEN TESTING GOES AWRY

Unfortunately, even when you have done your best to obtain a good assessment, there can be problems. You may disagree with the evaluation results or may feel that the examiner really did not understand your child. Don't despair! Your child needs you to continue to advocate for her. If the evaluation was done through her public school, it may make sense to hire a private psychologist or educational advocate to review the results and, perhaps, conduct further testing. If her testing was done privately, first discuss your concerns with the professional you worked with. If that does not result in a satisfactory outcome, seek another opinion. In some cases, you may need to consider that the assessment was accurate and you are having difficulty accepting the information you received. If you disagree with the evaluation conducted at your child's school, you have the right to request an independent educational evaluation (IEE) or additional testing.

have to accept the results or follow the recommendations. If they choose to reject the outside evaluation or its recommendations, they should provide the reasons for doing so in writing.

Now What?

We have a way of describing assessments that end up in a file cabinet of the evaluator or in a pile on a parent's desk, with no other resulting action. We call this "So What Testing." Testing is useful only if it leads you to a clear understanding of how to help. When your child is having trouble, you want to understand what you can do! The interpretive session and the written report should directly address what needs to be done for your child.

Figuring out who should get copies of the results, how much information to share, and what kinds of follow-up services you need should all be part of the discussion after the evaluation. For example, attending school meetings is an add-on service that you may need from your evaluator. Certainly, the evaluator should be able to offer recommendations for other professionals in the community who can provide the services you need. This is why we prefer that the evaluation be done locally by a provider in your community, unless no such option is available.

7

AD/HD, Learning Disabilities, and Other Conditions Associated with Executive Dysfunction

➢ Executive dysfunction sometimes occurs without any other disorder. Executive dysfunction alone can be viewed as a performance disability that can be just as problematic as AD/HD or learning disabilities.

➢ All children with AD/HD have executive weaknesses although the specific profiles vary.

➢ Many kids with executive dysfunction also have specific learning disabilities, meaning that they have unexpected difficulty learning in some specific *content* area (e.g., reading or math). However, some kids with weakness in executive functions have academic problems that are a result of their difficulties with the *process* of learning and performance. It can be hard to distinguish between these two causes of learning problems.

➢ Kids with autism spectrum disorders (ASD) typically have a weakness in cognitive flexibility.

➢ Executive weaknesses are common in children and adolescents with a range of neurodevelopmental, psychiatric, and medical disorders.

Remember that some kids are disorganized, or have other executive skill weaknesses, and nothing more. We do not mean to minimize the impact of these weaknesses by saying that these kids *only* have executive weaknesses. The "only" is used as a qualifier because for many other people, problems with executive skills are part of a larger picture of AD/HD, learning disabilities, or other disorders.

As we hope we have made clear already, we have seen in our daily work that executive weaknesses alone can be quite problematic. Dr. Martha Bridge Denckla was the first neuroscientist to describe executive dysfunction as a performance disability. Similar to children or adolescents with a specific reading learning disability or a clear deficit in language skills, Dr. Denckla realized that students who struggle with disorganization and other executive weaknesses have a disability that is apparent in their actual work output and ability to perform consistently. In her pioneering clinical work and research, she learned how these weaknesses can have a profound effect on daily life and on school achievement, even for gifted children. However, for many individuals, executive weaknesses are compounded by other conditions.

Diagnostics aside, the strategies for managing executive weaknesses in this book are not specific to any disorder, and we hope that you find them helpful regardless of whether your child has received any specific diagnosis.

Attention-Deficit/Hyperactivity Disorder (AD/HD)

Let us be clear: If a child or adolescent has AD/HD, he experiences some executive function weaknesses. Although each person has a different profile of strengths and weaknesses, delays or deficits in executive functioning are always present in people with AD/HD.

Here's where things get confusing. While all people with AD/HD have some degree of executive weakness, the reverse is not true. Not all individuals with executive dysfunction have AD/HD. Some kids and adults have notable executive dysfunction without clear attention deficits or characteristics that fit neatly into any diagnostic category.

Problems with executive functioning are a core deficit in AD/HD, and many experts in the field, including Drs. Thomas Brown and Russell Barkley, recommend reconceptualizing the disorder to reflect this. In fact, Dr. Brown has further suggested that executive deficits co-occur with many common psychiatric disorders.

Remember that diagnostic terms and classification systems change over time as we learn more about the nature of a disorder. In our current diagnostic system (DSM-IV-TR), there are several subtypes of Attention-Deficit/Hyperactivity Disorder. These subtypes of attention disorders are all categorized under the diagnostic label AD/HD. But there is more! In the formal classification system, there is always a comma after the AD/HD label. It is that which comes after the comma that gives us more specific information about the subtype.

When people think of AD/HD, they generally conjure up an image of a hyper kid. However, researchers and clinicians have learned over the years that this is only one of the possible forms of attention disorders. Some children do not have hyperactivity and are classified with AD/HD, Predominantly Inattentive Type (often referred to as ADD). As the name implies, these kids tend to be inattentive. They tend to have trouble getting started with tasks and sustaining their effort, and they may be seen as spacey or often daydreaming. Disorganization is a common characteristic. A frequent parent and teacher complaint is that the child has completed his work but then left it in his backpack, forgetting to hand it in. In the clinical literature, people with this diagnosis have been described as having a "sluggish cognitive tempo."

The Hyperactive-Impulsive Type of AD/HD includes kids whose predominant problems are impulsiveness and overactivity, the "hyper kid." These are the kids whose engines always seem to be racing and who act first and think later.

The Combined Type of AD/HD describes kids who have elements of both of the subtypes outlined above. So, they have inattention, distractibility, and problems with hyperactivity and impulse control.

Finally, when a youngster has notable difficulties with attention, impulse control, and/or hyperactivity but not to the extent or with the frequency that meets criteria for one of the three subtypes, they may be diagnosed with AD/HD, Not Otherwise Specified (NOS).

Drs. Kathleen Nadeau and Patricia Quinn have highlighted the special needs of girls and women with AD/HD. Since they may be less disruptive than some of their male peers, the inattention and executive deficits of girls may not be as readily noticeable, particularly in the elementary grades. However, these girls may be quietly struggling, and their difficulties often become more noticeable when they experience the increased demands of middle and high school.

Many children with AD/HD benefit from treatment with medication. While we understand that many parents have fears and misgivings about the use of medication for attention disorders, these can be a critical component of the treatment plan for many people. Stimulant medications, particularly, have been the target of much negative press over the years. We encourage parents to educate themselves about the pros and cons of medication and to carefully look for well-reasoned information based on scientifically sound research. People who write about medications for AD/HD often have strong opinions, not always based on facts. Consult with your pediatrician or an experienced child and adolescent psychiatrist to determine what is best for your child.

With or without medication, however, knowing how to help your AD/HD child with executive functioning is very important. Although medication often improves attention, decreases impulsivity, and quiets hyperactivity, the other executive functions are not usually notably improved. This may contribute to frustration as a student has better focus but still cannot remember to turn in his homework. That is what the interventions in this book are about.

Learning Disabilities (LD)

The term learning disability (LD) refers to an unexpected difficulty in learning some specific academic skill or set of skills. It is unexpected because individuals with learning disabilities have all the intelligence and instruction they need to learn, yet they have chronic difficulties in mastering reading, math, writing, and/or spelling. These difficulties are believed to have a neurological origin that is subtle and not yet fully understood. Like AD/HD, learning disabilities sometimes run in families.

In her work, Dr. Denckla noticed that many of the students with learning disabilities that she evaluated had some characteristics in common with kids with AD/HD. What they had in common was weakness in executive functioning, and she called this shared deficit the overlap zone.

Why do folks with executive weaknesses have difficulty with academics? Sometimes, they have both executive weakness and a co-occurring learning disability. However, the very characteristics that we define as weak executive skills lead a child to have trouble—not with the content of the material to be learned, but with the process of learning or of performing in the classroom. Let's looks at some real-life examples to make this distinction clearer.

Alan is a second grader who appears to his parents and teachers to be quite bright. While Alan loves math and science and does well in those subjects, he complains that he hates reading. He is reluctant to work on reading tasks and has been since he first started reading instruction. Alan has particular difficulty sounding out words and his reading is very slow and labored. He enjoys stories when others read to him, but otherwise he sticks with picture books that seem better suited to younger children.

Brianna is also struggling with reading. She tends to be inconsistent, sometimes reading the very same words differently within one sentence. She tends to look at the first letters of a word and then guess at the rest, and she reads very quickly. Sometimes, if you ask her to tell you about what she just read, she can't remember. However, when she reads with someone who encourages her to slow down and to look at the whole of each word, she does fine. With prompting to think about what she reads and with encouragement to look back at the text, she demonstrates good comprehension.

In the examples above, we see profiles of two children who both have problems with reading that affect their school performance. However, Alan's difficulties are due to a specific learning disability in reading. Brianna's reading problems have all the red flags of executive dysfunction; she can actually read well but her problems with attention to detail, working memory, and pacing mirror the problems she has in many other areas.

It can be difficult to distinguish between these two different reasons for academic difficulty. However, since understanding the nature of the problem affects our understanding of how to help, it is a very important distinction to make. If your child undergoes testing, the psychologist or other evaluator will help you figure out if there is a primary problem with reading skills and/or if attention and executive function weaknesses are impeding his reading achievement. If testing has not been completed, you may want to talk with your child's teachers to help determine where the reading process is breaking down.

Reading Disorder

A variety of different cognitive processes are involved in the ability to read accurately, fluently, and with good comprehension. When any one of these cognitive processes breaks down, a disability may be the result. Some children have difficulty with hearing the individual sounds or units of sound in language. Some have difficulty relating the sounds to letters. Some children have difficulty recognizing letter patterns. Others have trouble with comprehension with or without decoding problems. (Decoding refers to the ability to "sound out" words.)

As Dr. Denckla noted, research has shown that many kids with reading disabilities have characteristics that overlap with executive dysfunction. Common overlaps include: weaknesses in working memory, trouble with retrieval efficiency (meaning that it is difficult to pull information from long-term memory when it is needed), and difficulty distinguishing between minor details and the big picture. Even when specific reading deficits are remediated, attention and executive weaknesses can continue to compromise academic functioning.

Some kids with executive weaknesses do not have a separate reading disorder at all. As in Brianna's case, some children are impulsive and tend to read much too quickly, not absorbing the material adequately. They may have trouble matching their level of effort and reading rate to the level of difficulty of the material. For example, reading a celebrity news magazine and reading *The Odyssey* require significantly different levels of attention and depth of processing. Although most children figure this out on their own, some need explicit instruction in how to match their effort and depth of processing to the material they are reading.

For children and adolescents who have reading disabilities, there are a range of research-supported interventions that are often effective in building improved reading skills. These can be implemented at school or by a private tutor, and need to be provided by educational professionals who have specialized training and experience.

For kids with weak phonics skills, the interventions usually involve multisensory (visual, auditory, and kinesthetic) instruction and practice to improve the ability to quickly sound out words.

Other interventions target reading rate and fluency for those who have mastered most of the basics of reading but lack the rapid and automatic reading skills of their peers.

Some students with reading disorders struggle primarily with reading comprehension. For them, the goal is to teach cognitive strategies to improve how actively they are processing what they read. These interventions may include instruction and practice with summarizing, highlighting/note-taking, and other ways of helping the student understand and organize what he is reading.

The other primary means of helping kids with significant reading problems is to make the actual act of reading easier. Although most of us do best with silent reading, some people benefit from reading aloud or being read to (this means they will need to take tests at school in a separate room). When a student in mid-elementary school or above has to work hard just to figure out the individual words, his comprehension suffers, and reading is more effortful for him than for his peers. Recorded books or computer-based programs that read to the child with a reading disability can be very helpful so that he doesn't have to decode and can concentrate on understanding the material.

Many of the techniques that are helpful for kids with reading disorders can also be beneficial for students whose reading performance is compromised by executive dysfunction. For example, Matt has average reading skills but quickly loses focus when reading and has trouble determining the most important points in a textbook chapter. He listens to most of his textbooks on a CD and asks his parents or tutor to read some material that is not available in digital format. This promotes his concentration and allows him to review parts of the material he does not understand after one presentation.

If your child has difficulty reading due to executive weaknesses, you will find strategies to address these issues in the second half of the book (Chapters 14 and 15).

Mathematics Disorder

A specific learning disability in math means that the person has difficulty understanding basic math concepts and/or learning to solve arithmetic problems. As with reading disorders, some kids have a primary math disability and others have problems primarily with the executive skills needed for math.

Math can be difficult for those with executive dysfunction because it often requires multi-tasking and managing details. Weak executive functioning may show up as mistakes that are a result of inadequate attention to the operational sign on computation problems and other seemingly careless errors. If a student makes a mistake on any part of a multi-step problem, the answer will be wrong!

The child may perform better on more challenging problems because the task difficulty slows down the analysis process and keeps him from making the seemingly silly errors he makes on easier problems.

Math problems, particularly oral problems, often require students to hold information in mind to carry into a later step in solving the problem. Some kids with memory inefficiencies struggle to learn basic math facts. Kids with poor self-monitoring may not recognize when their answer doesn't make sense. When provided with extraneous information in a word problem, some kids with organizational difficulties have a hard time focusing in on the important details.

Although math learning disabilities are still not as well researched as reading disabilities, there are many trusted interventions that are helpful in remediating weaknesses. Multisensory approaches (strategies that connect new learning with input from the eyes, ears, voice, and/or hands) are often used to promote mastery and reinforce math facts. A skilled teacher or tutor will help a student develop a systematic approach or template for completing math problems. Again, many of the techniques that benefit kids with mathematics disorders are also appropriate for students whose executive weaknesses impair their math performance. Sometimes it is helpful to teach the child to highlight or circle math procedure signs (+, -) or to read the problem aloud before he begins working to help prevent "careless" errors. You will find more suggestions in the chapters on interventions for children who need help controlling impulsive behavior, managing weak working memory, and monitoring their own behavior.

Disorder of Written Expression (Writing LD)

Writing is an incredibly complex task that requires:

- getting started;
- the physical act of writing or keyboarding;
- using correct punctuation and capitalization;
- spelling words correctly;
- writing in sentences;
- following oral or written directions;
- staying on-track and being organized;
- working within time limits; and
- figuring out when one has done sufficient research and written enough.

Kids with problems with written expression can have difficulty because of the mechanics of writing (spelling, grammar, punctuation), the formulation of ideas, and organization of their responses, or all three. There are also plenty of students who struggle with the physical act of handwriting. (There is a separate term for people with handwriting difficulties: developmental coordination disorder or dysgraphia.)

Many kids with executive weaknesses have trouble with written expression. There is simply too much to keep track of! Mel Levine, M.D., in his book *The Myth of Laziness*, describes writing as "the largest orchestra a kid's mind has to conduct." He understands that many kids have trouble with the executive demands of writing. They may simplify the task by writing less complex and/or fewer sentences than required. These minimalists are often overwhelmed by the writing process and have increasing difficulty as they proceed through school. In our experience, it is not unusual for kids with writing learning disabilities to be brilliant poets and do well on creative writing tasks while demonstrating significant impairment when required to complete more structured writing assignments. Others do fine with factually-based writing but struggle with creative writing tasks.

Children or adolescents with writing disabilities often benefit from special education services or working with a specially-trained tutor. They need explicit instruction in how to do research, decide on a topic, structure sentences, organize their work, and proofread. Keyboarding instruction and the use of voice recognition software may be very useful for students with slow or poor handwriting.

The overlap between interventions for specific learning disabilities and executive weakness is nowhere more apparent than with written expression. Many kids with writing problems have trouble with initiation. It is often helpful to allow these students to dictate some or all of an assignment.

For students who have difficulty with organizing and planning their written work, there are many useful software programs available that allow a child to generate ideas and organize information using visual techniques, such as mind-mapping and graphic organizers.

Kids with weak self-monitoring skills need to learn to review their work by reading it aloud or using supportive software, as it is very hard to "catch" errors when reading silently. If you are the parent of a child or adolescent with a disorder of written expression or executive weaknesses, you or a tutor/coach may need to continue to serve a quality control function with regard to editing written work.

For students whose writing problems are secondary to executive weaknesses, review some of the many suggestions in the second half of this book. You may be particularly interested in the chapters that focus on how to help children with problems with working memory and with planning/organizational skills.

Students with learning disabilities and/or executive dysfunction are at notable risk for academic underachievement and developing secondary emotional, behavioral, and self-esteem problems when they do not receive appropriate supports. There are many local and national ad-

CASE STUDY

Simone is a fifth grader who has been diagnosed with AD/HD (predominantly inattentive type) and a reading disorder (dyslexia). Although she has benefited greatly from intervention to improve her decoding skills, she remains a slow reader and below average at spelling. Simone also struggles with concentration. She is not impulsive; in fact, she tends to work and process information slowly. Simone's strengths include her strong intelligence and exceptional persistence—she will keep working until the job is done! However, with each new grade, her reading and attention weaknesses make it harder and harder for her to keep up with her peers. Although she doesn't complain, she spends an average of three hours each day on homework while most of her friends are done in an hour or less. Simone often has to re-read information both due to working memory and attentional inefficiencies. Given her fatigue at the end of the day and the energy and time needed to complete homework, she has stopped participating in extracurricular activities, like gymnastics and choir.

Simone's mother is understandably concerned about how her daughter will manage the increased demands of middle school. She requested an evaluation by a psychologist in order to help her daughter plan for this important transition. Simone's many strengths (including her pleasant disposition and tremendous work ethic) were identified along with her weaknesses in reading rate, phonological processing, spelling, working memory, planning, and organization. Recommendations included specific remediation in reading, experimenting with assistive technology (e.g., software that will read to her, digital books), modifications and accommodations in the classroom, and a medical consultation to consider the pros and cons of a trial of medication to address inattention. Her mother was advised to share the evaluation results with the school and to request appropriate accommodations and modifications.

vocacy organizations that provide information and support to parents of children and adolescents with learning disabilities and AD/HD. Further, we provide specific suggestions in later chapters to address weaknesses in initiation, working memory, planning, organization, and self-monitoring that may be apparent in students with learning disabilities.

In addition to providing specialized interventions to build academic skills, an important way of helping kids with specific learning disabilities is through reasonable accommodations and modifications. These are designed to "even the playing field" and include adjustments to instruction, testing, and expectations. For example, a student with a reading disorder may be allowed extra time for tests and have individualized expectations for homework (e.g., completing as much reading as possible within one hour rather than being expected to complete a set number of pages). Remember that expectations need to be revisited regularly so that we are promoting growth and independence while still providing the supports and accommodations that are needed.

Autism Spectrum Disorders (ASD)

Autism and its variants have received much media attention over the last few years. There is a broad range, or spectrum, of this disorder. Children with autism spectrum disorders (ASD) have delays in the development of reciprocal social interactions and language skills, and present with ritualistic, repetitive activities or interests. Many people with ASD have a preoccupation with very specific things, such as the Civil War, emergency vehicles, or train schedules, and many demonstrate idiosyncratic behaviors including repetitive speech or habits. Asperger syndrome is a milder form of ASD in which most language skills develop normally.

Social characteristics of people with ASD include difficulty interpreting the unspoken rules of social interaction. The normal give-and-take of peer interactions requires an increasingly nuanced understanding of what drives human behavior. Particularly in adolescence, children need to attend to verbal and nonverbal cues to figure out how other people are feeling. Problems in this arena may be compounded by executive weaknesses in self-monitoring and impulse control.

Most kids with ASD also have trouble with flexible thinking and problem-solving. They tend to be somewhat rigid and have trouble with transitions and adjusting to change. Furthermore, these children may have trouble generalizing, or transferring previous knowledge and skills to new situations. Since people with ASD tend to become anxious and overwhelmed when faced with unfamiliar demands or situations, these situations may require significant external support. Even small environmental changes can result in emotional and cognitive overload.

The later chapters on impulse control, cognitive flexibility, and self-monitoring will be of particular help to those parents with children on the autism spectrum. Additionally, there is a plethora of books in the current market devoted to intervention strategies geared specifically to this audience. Some are included in the reference section at the back of this book.

One important issue in advocating for and supporting your child with ASD is helping his teachers, coaches, and therapists understand the role of executive function and other cognitive differences in his behavior and response to stress. For example, Cheryl, a ten-year-old with Asperger syndrome, becomes extremely upset whenever there is a substitute teacher or other unexpected change in her school routine. If she cannot complete classwork or does not participate in a class discussion, these should be interpreted within the context of her ASD and related cognitive rigidity. For a typically-developing peer, a lack of work completion may warrant a behavioral consequence that would not be appropriate for Cheryl.

Other Conditions Often Associated with Executive Function Weaknesses

Although outside the scope of this book, we want you to know that executive function delays and deficits are commonly experienced by children and adolescents with a range of other neurodevelopmental, psychiatric, and medical conditions. These include nonverbal learning disability (NLD), Tourette syndrome (TS), seizure disorders, traumatic brain injury (TBI), and sleep disorders and deprivation. A number of genetic syndromes also involve executive weaknesses as part of the profile, including Fragile X, Velocardiofacial syndrome (VCFS), and Turner syndrome.

Some degree of executive dysfunction is typically found in children and adolescents with a psychiatric disorder, such as an anxiety disorder (including obsessive-compulsive disorder, or OCD), depression, bipolar disorder (and the newly proposed severe mood dysregulation disorder), or a psychotic disorder, as well as kids experiencing notable emotional distress due to situational stressors.

Finally, children and adolescents who experienced early abuse, neglect, and/or institutional care are at significant risk for difficulties with self-regulation and other executive skills.

Wrap-Up

People often ask us how many children and adolescents have delays or weaknesses in executive functioning. That question is essentially impossible to answer because there are many developmental and acquired conditions that include executive function weaknesses. This is further complicated by the comorbidity among these conditions (that is our clinical term for the overlap between different types of neurodevelopmental disabilities).

We want to emphasize the need to analyze and understand each student's profile in order to determine how to help him rather than relying on diagnoses and labels. Telling us that a fourteen-year-old has Asperger syndrome does not tell us about his personality, information-processing skills, academic functioning, interests, family and school environments, or specific executive skills. While such terms are often needed to obtain appropriate supports and services at school, they are not sufficient to help us plan effective interventions and supports. As many parents have helped us appreciate, their child's diagnosis often tells us little about his strengths and needs.

Part 2
WHAT YOU CAN DO ABOUT IT

8

How to Help: An Overview

THE BASICS

➤ Our approach to building executive competence involves balancing two goals: helping the child manage demands in the short run and building independent skills for long-term self-management.

➤ All short-term strategies are designed to lighten the load on the executive system.

➤ Long-term strategies focus on strengthening the executive system and building a repertoire of effective self-management skills to compensate for executive weaknesses.

➤ Figuring out how to help begins with clearly and specifically defining the problems and deciding where to start.

➤ Interventions do not come in a one-size-fits-all package. They must be tailored to the child and the setting.

Yes, help is (finally) on the way! How can we improve the chances that children and adolescents with executive weaknesses meet with success in life? In this chapter, we lay out a general approach to helping your child. In the next chapter, we provide some basic principles of behavior change to guide your treatment planning. The chapters that follow provide specific strategies, or interventions, that we have pulled together from our own experience and from other clinicians, to target various areas of weakness within the executive system.

The Two-Pronged Approach

Parents and teachers have two primary roles in helping kids with executive weaknesses. The first is to help children to be successful in their daily lives. The second is to teach the skills and approaches that allow the children to be independent in the long run. If we only provide temporary supports, we may be reinforcing overdependence and learned helplessness. However, if we don't offer adequate short-term support while our kids build better executive skills, they may experience a range of negative academic and emotional consequences with long-term effects.

Short-Term Goals: Building a Prosthetic Environment

Just as we provide prostheses for someone who cannot walk otherwise, children with executive weakness need adults to adapt their environment and tasks when they do not yet have sufficient executive competence to succeed on their own. For this reason, Dr. Russell Barkley refers to the process of accommodating kids as building a "prosthetic environment."

External support, limits, and supervision can all be types of prostheses. The supports that are needed change over time and, hopefully, eventually not be needed at all.

All of these short-term strategies are designed to lighten the load on the executive system. We do this by modifying the nature of the task and/or by providing support and supplementing the child's executive system. This allows the child to be more successful in daily life. Although we call these strategies short-term, it is important to understand that many kids may need support for years, not weeks or months, with the goal of having them eventually learn how to independently manage tasks and demands.

Jim is a child who has trouble organizing and planning written reports. He has trouble getting started and monitoring his written work for correct spelling, punctuation, and capitalization. Jim's father has tried many times to help him develop an outline and use a proofreading checklist but nothing seems to work. Jim is working with a writing tutor and developing an approach that works for him. He uses writing software to produce a graphic organizer (visual display of what he will write about) and then uses another program that reads his work aloud so that he can catch mistakes. He still needs his tutor or father to proofread lengthier or more important papers so that he receives support as he continues to build his writing and executive skills.

A prosthetic environment provides opportunities for children to continue to take part in experiences that further development. Consider how a child with executive dysfunction might benefit from the sense of belonging and the outdoor group activities that characterize participation in Boy Scouts and Girl Scouts. Even children who have difficulties initiating and independently organizing the projects required to earn badges can get a lot out of the group. Accommodations in the form of extra support from a parent and from the troop leader allow the child to be a part of the many developmental experiences that joining this extracurricular group can provide.

Finally, and perhaps most importantly, helping a child to be more successful on a daily basis reduces the risk of serious secondary problems, such as depression, anxiety, and low self-esteem. These secondary problems can arise from the constant demoralization caused by failure to meet expectations day after day. In addition to increased vulnerability to emotional difficulties, people with weaknesses in impulse control, monitoring, and judgment are at higher risk for substance abuse and risky behavior. We encourage parents to enforce tighter limits and to provide closer supervision for adolescents with these risk factors.

Parents who provide appropriate supports for their children with executive weaknesses may be accused of trying to protect them from the realities of life. We think it makes sense to provide a level of protection and a buffer from demands when a child does not yet have the skills to independently manage them. If we do not provide this, even very bright, talented kids may come to view themselves as incompetent and ineffective. Depending upon temperament, they may become overly self-critical or give up due to their inconsistent performance. Without appropriate expectations and supports to even the playing field, these youngsters may experience academic underachievement, underemployment, and interpersonal problems.

By experiencing success when the supports are in place, children learn that it is possible to succeed. With the guidance of adults, children can begin to understand the kinds of supports they need and where to find them so that, over time, they can learn to put these into place and use them as appropriate.

For most of the people we have worked with, the self-awareness and maturity to recognize the need for help and to seek appropriate support comes late in the game. Often, parental guidance continues to be needed into high school and, for some, into the college and young adult years. This guidance must be balanced with the need to allow the emotional and practical independence that our adolescents and young adults are seeking. That is no easy balance! It is important that adults evaluate on an ongoing basis whether they can scale back their direct involvement. In Chapter 10 we discuss ways to accomplish this balance.

Going the Distance: Building Executive Skills

If we only focus on short-term goals with our kids, then we are only doing half of our job. It is also important to provide the explicit teaching and the practice vital to increasing their executive competence. Building skills can be done with help from parents, teachers, tutors, therapists, and other important adults.

Long-term interventions focus on strengthening the executive system and building a repertoire of effective self-management skills to compensate for executive weaknesses. These interventions allow our children to be competent as they move out into the world on their own.

One of the most effective ways of building executive skills is by developing habits and routines that eventually become automatic. Building habits requires repetition, repetition, and more repetition. Here's the good news: Once you no longer have to think about doing something, you largely bypass the executive system. Here's the bad news: It really does require repetition, ad nauseam, for kids with executive weaknesses to internalize these behaviors. Remember, this is not a knowledge problem. As with adults who are trying to change their behavior (have you ever tried to lose weight?), kids often know what they should do, but tend to revert to their old ways. Once behaviors become automatic, they no longer require conscious effort. Until that point, independent performance of the desired behavior is likely to be inconsistent. This is why it is so important to provide the prosthetic environment while the skills are still developing.

USING HABITS AND ROUTINES TO MANAGE YOUR LIFE

Let's move away from talking about kids for just a minute and look at the role of habits and routines in our adult lives. When you walk in the door to your house, where do you put your keys? When you are ready to leave the house again, do you have to look for them? Most adults have a designated place for their keys, having learned by experience the importance of putting them in the same place every time. Are you a hook person? Or a basket or table person? Whatever your special place, it is probably so automatic at this point that there is no effort involved in this small detail of your day.

Now, if you move to a new house, you will likely be disoriented until you build new habits. You will once again have to think about your keys. As simple as it sounds, building habits and routines is one of the most powerful ways to manage repetitive tasks efficiently. Routines can be applied to much more complex tasks, as well, such as schoolwork and study habits. The more you can help your child to develop habits and routines that make sense for her, the more likely she is to be able to manage demands independently.

As children get older, it is increasingly important that they learn how to manage daily life demands and know what to do to compensate for their executive weaknesses. We must actively engage them in experimenting with various strategies to see what works and suits their particular style. For any given problem situation, it is critical to approach interventions with the mindset that we must build in both short- and long-term ways to help the child so that we are doing both important jobs.

Designing Interventions

The Detective Phase

Designing interventions begins with a detective process. Success at any given task generally involves a whole chain of behaviors. If a child is not succeeding, we must figure out exactly what link in the chain is missing. For a kid with multiple weaknesses (lots of missing links), planning and delivering interventions can be more challenging.

Kevin often gets low grades in school because he does not turn in homework. In an interview with Kevin and his parents, it was determined that he does not write down homework assignments consistently. He also forgets to bring home his textbooks.

Debbie also gets low grades due to failure to turn in homework. She writes down all of her assignments and she generally finishes some of her work each night. However, she tends to underestimate how long assignments will take and so she starts too late to complete the work.

Clearly, understanding where in the cycle the process breaks down is an important first step. We use this knowledge to target the problem. We can then address the problem using specific strategies. For example, teachers may comment that a student needs to hand in assignments on time. However, turning in homework is a process that requires bringing the assignment home, completing it, putting the assignment in a backpack, and bringing it to school and to class, etc. Once a teacher identifies clearly the step in the process at which the child falters, the teacher can develop specific target goals, e.g., "Kevin will record daily and long-term assignments in his agenda book. In the margin next to each assignment, he will list all books needed to complete the work. Kevin's agenda book will be initialed for completeness by each teacher on a daily basis." For Debbie, supports and strategies are quite different. "Debbie will meet with her advisor each Monday and will develop and record a plan for completing all assignments and studying for tests. The written plan will be provided to her parents who will use verbal prompts if she does not check in and show her progress by eight o'clock each evening."

Creativity at Work

The first step in helping kids is to define the problem or the behavior to be changed. This often means figuring out what is interfering with success or development or what is different about a child that is causing difficulty (See Chapter 6, Assessment: Figuring Out What's Wrong). We can be most helpful when we specifically identify behaviors (e.g., "she loses her assignment book") rather than focusing on broad characteristics (e.g., "she is forgetful"). Once we have a target behavior defined, there are many different ways to intervene. There is no one set of interventions that suits all children or all settings.

An important part of helping disorganized kids is prioritizing what is getting in their way of academic or social adjustment. For example, although it may drive you crazy as a parent, her messy room may be less of a priority than her disorganized backpack. In order to be effective and supportive, we need to work on one goal at a time without becoming overwhelmed or sidetracked by blaming or frustration. Tackling one skill or issue at a time is not only practical, it also models how kids can best build strategies and skills.

Interventions are most likely to be effective when the child or adolescent plays an active role. Inviting collaboration can be challenging, particularly when adolescents are doing their best to separate from their parents. Sometimes the most unconventional approaches are the most effective. If a disorganized student remembers her binder because she puts it next to her lunch in the refrigerator, that is fine as long as it works for her!

This is why our work is exciting and fresh! The number of possible interventions is limited only by our ability to think outside the box. This is particularly true when trying to help kids who don't even know there is a box!

In the next few chapters, we present some of the interventions that we have found helpful for children with whom we have worked. Our goal, though, is for you to understand the principles well enough that you can design interventions that work for the specific challenges you and your child face. So, at the beginning of each intervention chapter, we list the general principles we apply to build better functioning in that particular area of executive weakness.

A FEW MORE THINGS ABOUT INTERVENTIONS

Interventions are not:
- Doing everything for the child
- Excuses for inadequate effort or bad behavior
- Praising or rewarding all behavior

Interventions often:
- Involve setting different expectations for a given child
- Change as a child grows up and encounters new tasks and demands
- Require ongoing adjustment.

9

Behavior Change in a Nutshell

THE BASICS

> Kids are most likely to be successful when we teach using real-life tasks rather than trying to teach skills in the abstract.

> Teaching new skills to children and adolescents with executive skill weaknesses may require a different approach than other children. Natural consequences and typical behavioral interventions may not be effective.

> Change generally happens in small steps, not in giant leaps. It is important to recognize the effort and accomplishment involved in even small steps if they are moving in the right direction.

If you are going to be the architect of your child's intervention plan, or even just an informed reviewer of the plan, then you need to know some basic principles of behavior change. Here are some of the major principles that guide us.

Use Real Life to Teach

Skills learned in the context of real-life activities generally have better sticking power than skills taught in the abstract. For example, helping a child with the planning and organizing for a school or home project is more effective than a study skills class in the summer that teaches basic principles of how one organizes things. Kids learn something from those classes, but there are some real pitfalls to the classroom approach. The most important thing to know is that applying the skills does not necessarily follow from learning them in an isolated environment. It is the daily application of skills and tools that forges good habits over time, and that is where real life offers the best opportunities.

Take a Teaching versus a Punishing Approach

Remember that the origins of the word discipline come from the Latin word that means "to teach." While thoughtful punishments certainly have a role in raising children, they are useless if the child does not know and have the ability to perform the desired behavior. You would be up in arms if your child's first grade teacher yelled at him for not knowing how to read. Instead, you expect the child to be offered instruction geared to teaching the foundation skills and then moving forward to more advanced lessons as the child's abilities progress. Do the same at home. Teach your child, in very specific behavioral terms, what is expected of him. "You need to go back and pick up your coat and hang it on the hook," is much more effective (and respectful) than, "I've told you not to be such a slob!"

In addition to the practical and self-esteem considerations, using punishment with kids with working memory weaknesses and trouble delaying gratification may simply be unrealistic and ineffective. We understand how frustrating it is to see your child make the same mistakes over and over again, but lectures, threats, and reliance only on negative consequences are usually ineffective in building skills and changing behavior in the long run.

Collaborate with Your Child

Your child is most likely to be successful in making changes when he is an active participant in developing goals and deciding how to reach them. Consider the child's ideas and input and reinforce the child for being willing to experiment with a range of approaches. As children get older, they are better able to generate and evaluate possible ways of building habits and changing behavior. However, even younger children often respond positively to being asked to help with problem-solving and monitoring how things are going. Kids can also help us understand what is getting in their way.

Focus on the Desired Outcome

Focus on helping the child to achieve a relevant, meaningful behavior rather than focusing on what is getting in the way. For example, squirmy and distractible kids often have trouble completing their schoolwork. Adults may assume that the problem with work completion is that the child needs to sit still and keep his attention on the worksheet. So, the child might be rewarded for sitting quietly in his seat and keeping his eyes on the paper. Unfortunately, that does not mean that the child is getting more work done!

If you want a child to complete more work, then focus on the goal of getting more work done! Now, there may need to be some other changes to allow that to happen. Ben may need to be moved away from the kid who encourages misbehavior. Ana may need to get up and walk around for a few minutes; she may be asked to hand out papers, run an errand, or be allowed to get a drink of water. Peter's concentration and work completion may be enhanced by letting him suck on a hard candy, chew gum, or use a fidget toy such as a squishy ball or piece of clay. However, all of these approaches should be evaluated in the context of whether or not the child is getting more work done. After we clarify just what the goal is for any intervention, we creatively generate possible ways to meet the goal. Whenever we can elicit input and cooperation from the child, the child's chances of success increase greatly.

Raise the Stakes

Concrete rewards, point systems and the like are all aimed at increasing the importance of a behavior from the child's perspective. Kids don't necessarily see the value of what we are trying to teach them. And if they don't see the value, they aren't likely to put much effort toward a goal. So, sometimes we need to make the behavioral goal more important to the child by tying it to a reward, or tethering failure to perform the desired behavior to a loss of privileges. Positive reinforcement for a specific behavior shines a spotlight on the goal, and it helps the child to maintain interest and sustain effort.

We understand that many parents have concerns about bribing or rewarding kids for what they theoretically *should* be doing. However, if a child does not yet have sufficient skills to complete the task consistently and independently, using rewards can be very effective and appropriate in helping to build skills, routines, and habits. After all, most adults are motivated by earning a paycheck, even when they enjoy and value their work.

Reward Even Small Steps in the Right Direction

Change generally happens in small steps, not in one giant leap. It is important to recognize the effort and accomplishment involved in even small steps toward a goal. For example, Matt often ended up at soccer practice without his soccer bag. His Mom worked on helping him to develop a checklist of things that he needed to pack into the soccer bag and made a plan with him to put the bag into the car the night before practice. At first, Matt tended to rush the process by packing from memory and then tossing the bag into the car without double-checking that he had what he needed. His mother praised him for getting the bag to soccer practice, and then encouraged him to use his checklist, too, so that he would have all of the essentials for practice.

It is a basic principle of behavior change that any behavior followed by a positive result is more likely to recur, and any behavior followed by a negative result is less likely to recur. So, if Matt completed one step of the process, and his Mom yelled at him for not doing the other steps, can you see how that would discourage the small, but positive, change Matt had made?

Use "Tried and True" Behavior Modification Techniques

Behavior modification is the process of applying the basic principles of behavior change in a systematic and planned manner. When informal behavior modification techniques are insufficient to bring about desired behavior change, then more formal systems may need to be put into place. These systems are built on the same basic principles outlined above: Any behavior followed by a positive event is more likely to recur, and any behavior followed by a negative event is less likely to recur.

For many kids and teens, behavioral plans help to build confidence, as they provide concrete evidence of their own competence when they meet the standards. Further, parents and kids, themselves, are less likely to make global, negative attributions about behavior when they see success with some behaviors despite not meeting all the goals.

Behavioral plans range from simple agreements, targeting just a few behaviors, to comprehensive plans that lay out expectations for the whole of the day at school and/or home. The more comprehensive plans are helpful for children who are unable to regulate their behavior without step-by-step guidance. Some kids also need the concrete and immediate feedback that a detailed behavioral plan offers. The key here is matching a plan to your child.

Matching a plan to the individual also includes choosing age-appropriate rewards for older children and teens. Reward systems work best, in general, when the child or teen contributes to the design of the plan by considering both the behavioral expectations and the possible rewards for improved performance. This is particularly important for teens, who will need to consider with parents what rewards would be meaningful to them. Perhaps more cell phone time? Perhaps they could save up points for an outing? Likewise, they will need to have input as to what privileges will be docked if they do not meet the standards.

Many plans incorporate a menu of rewards, since working toward the same reward repeatedly becomes less appealing once the novelty wears off. Reward menus for more comprehensive plans include some choices that require fewer points, such as what might be earned in a single day, as well as choices that would require points to be saved over a longer period of time.

For children and teens having behavioral issues at school, it is important that parents and teachers collaborate so that there is consistency and communication from one setting to the other.

The overarching goal of any formal behavioral plan is for the person to perform the desired behaviors so reliably and consistently that the plan is no longer needed. For many older children and teens, earning their way off the system is the biggest reward of all!

You will notice that the use of basic principles of behavior change, in general, and explicit behavioral plans, specifically, is incorporated into the suggestions we provide in Chapters 11 through 16. We also include some books in our reference section that you can turn to if you want to read more about behavioral plans.

Trust Your Child's Own Developmental Urges

Developmental unfolding is a powerful phenomenon, and most children have a strong need to be competent. If you can move out of a punitive perspective and align yourself with the part of your child that wants to grow up and be successful, then you will have fewer power struggles.

Practice these words: "Wow, you do have a problem. What do you think you can do about it?" Apply as needed when your child forgets to bring his book home from school, arrives at the beach in the summer with no bathing suit, et cetera. Help with problem solving, as needed, rather than taking over the problem or getting stuck in chastising, lecturing, or punishing.

When Should You Allow Your Child to Experience Natural Consequences for His Behavior?

Allowing your child to experience natural consequences *can* be a very effective way to motivate behavior change. For example, when a teen calls a week ahead of time to invite a friend over, his planning and initiation may be reinforced by the desired natural consequence because the friend was free to come over. The issues get trickier when the natural consequences are negative. Since many children and adolescents with executive function weaknesses do not yet have the skills they need to independently perform the desired behaviors, learning from experience may not be as effective as it is for typically developing peers. In such situations, negative natural consequences may be, at best, discouraging, and, at worst, devastating to continued development and success.

At times, we advise parents to intervene so that their kids do *not* experience the natural consequences of their behavior. Determining when you should intervene in the cycle of behavior and natural consequences is closely tied to your ability to set realistic expectations.

As an example, let's consider the developmental task of learning to cross the street independently. We assume that almost all kids eventually are able to cross the street without a parent present. This requires considerable executive skills as not all drivers stop at stop signs and the child needs to be able to judge if a vehicle is far enough away to allow time to safely cross. All kids quickly learn the rule for street crossing: "Stop, look both ways, cross if it is clear." However, being able to recite the rule does not mean that a child is ready to perform this behavior. Is there a universal age at which all kids can cross the street? Of course not! Perhaps we should tell seven-year-old Jon, "Your brother crossed the street when he was seven, so we know you can do it too!" Some kids master this skill at seven, while others do not do so until age ten. (There are even some teenagers we worry about!) Now, the natural consequence of failure to cross the street according to the rules is simply too steep a price to let a child go if they are not ready, so we take an active role to make sure the child is safe.

Just as we would not expect a child to cross the street without a parent before he is ready, we should not expect that a child can independently complete a project, get ready for the day, or plan for the coming week before these skills and habits are developed to an adequate level of mastery.

Sometimes, negative natural consequences can motivate a child to start applying strategies he has been resistant to or even to seek new skills. For example, Matt might start using his checklist to pack up his soccer bag if he has to sit out a game or two because he did not bring his shin guards. However, when we consider whether or not to let a child suffer negative natural consequences, we must be attuned to two factors: whether success is within reasonable reaching distance, and the cost of experiencing the negative consequences.

Change Does Not Occur in a Smooth or Steady Uphill Manner

Expect slow progress with ups and downs along the way. If you have ever tried to lose weight, then you know how slow behavior change can be. If you have been successful at losing weight, you have learned to set realistic goals, to celebrate small victories, and to recover when you have a setback. These are principles that guide all behavior change. (And was it ever helpful to have someone chide or make fun of you when you had that piece of chocolate cake or skipped your aerobics class?)

Frustration and exhaustion are normal parts of the parenting experience (and the child experience). If you can accept that, then you will be better able to help your child and enjoy the progress along the way. Your understanding, encouragement, and support go a long way to help your child develop the executive skills necessary to manage as an adult.

10

If at First You Don't Succeed, Try a Few More Times Then...Change your Expectations!

- ➢ Knowing where to set the bar for a child or adolescent who is out of synch with peers is a challenging job.

- ➢ Setting realistic expectations requires careful observation of your child's performance and a willingness to frequently re-evaluate based on how things go.

- ➢ Setting the bar too high can be as detrimental as setting it too low.

- ➢ Expectations must be based upon the child's unique profile rather than on the child's age or grade.

- ➢ You may need to adjust the height of the bar.

Parenting is a tough, rewarding, always challenging twenty-four-hour-a-day job that, for most of us, extends well beyond our child's eighteenth birthday. We need to provide nurturance and support, and we need to help our kids develop into responsible, competent adults. For kids with weaknesses in executive functioning, the journey from childhood to adulthood can be rocky. As their peers are handling increasingly complex tasks with greater independence, the child with executive weaknesses may continue to rely heavily on adult-provided structure and guidance. Knowing that your child is out of synch with the standard expectations for her age, what guidelines do you use to set expectations? How do you know if the expectations you have set are realistic for your child or teen's unique profile of strengths and weaknesses?

Don't Try to Keep Up with the Jones

The good news is that you are <u>the</u> expert on your child. You have watched your child grow over the years and understand what your child needs to thrive. In this world of experts of every type and more self-help books than you can shake a stick at, you possess unique wisdom and need to "trust your gut" when setting expectations. Don't listen to your co-worker or sister who says that your child will never develop responsibility unless you demand more of her. It is often the case for kids with executive weaknesses that the intent and desire are there to meet age-appropriate goals, but the means for achieving those goals is not. Remember, executive dysfunction is a performance disability: there is a gap between ability/knowledge and independent, consistent behavior.

The Limbo Game of Setting Expectations

How do you know where to set the bar for your child? Here are some clues to help you figure out if your expectations are where they should be:

Clue #1

If your child continually underperforms or does not meet expectations, it is likely that the bar is set too high. Please delete the word "should" from your vocabulary, at least when discussing your child. Also, the fact that you did something when you were the child's age, or that the child's older brother did not need extra help at the same task, is not the criterion to use to set the bar.

Clue #2

If the bar is set at the right height, your child should hit the goal more times than not. Don't expect your child to be 100 percent consistent; inconsistent behavior is the hallmark of executive dysfunction. This poses real challenges for setting fair expectations. It is like a trick; your child can amaze you with remembering to take out the garbage two out of seven times. If your child can do it sometimes, why can't you expect it to be done every time? Sometimes the child's essays are brilliant, while at other times it is hard to believe that the essay was written by the same child. And don't even get us started on the kids who spell a word three different ways within the same paper. Even though it's tempting to assume our kids are always trying to get away with something, more often than not they don't mean to be inconsistent. Look for the "hit" rate to improve with practice and repetition.

Clue #3

If everyone in your child's life seems to be in disagreement about how she's "doing," you may need to confer with a third party, perhaps by communicating with your child's teacher occasionally. Outside observations can provide a needed perspective on how your child is actually performing in the situation.

It is often instructive to ask students how they think they did on a paper or test. Many kids with problems in the executive system are very poor judges of their performance because they think they put forth adequate effort and did what was asked of them. Imagine how discouraging it is to believe that you studied hard but received a "D" because of inadvertently skipped items and seemingly careless errors. So, don't assume that your child is avoiding telling you the truth on purpose. The child may be clueless! (That is not to say that kids with executive dysfunction do not sometimes try to cover their tracks, just as their peers do.)

Clue #4

If you feel like you are on the brink of losing touch with your child, consider that your child may be having difficulty living up to expectations. Often kids with executive weaknesses cope with embarrassment and shame by pretending that they just don't care about school or whatever standards you have set. This is a self-protective maneuver. It often feels more comfortable to say "I just didn't try" than to admit you tried and didn't succeed. This is particularly true for people with weak impulse control, who behave in ways they didn't intend and then have to deal with the consequences. Be cautious about assuming that your child really doesn't care about being successful. This may be the mask that the child wears to save face. Consider ways to bolster your child's success rate to see if that affects the child's behavior and attitude.

You may need to lower the bar just a bit to allow for more success. Sometimes simplifying your child's life by eliminating an activity or demand helps to relieve some of the pressure.

Sometimes your child needs more help in one particular area. At other times, the child may be overwhelmed trying to manage many demands. To bolster the success rate you can consider reducing the challenge level or adding more support. Let us offer two brief examples.

> *Tina, a third grader, was brought in for consultation due to increased stress that showed up as tearfulness, difficulty sleeping, and complaints about going to school that she had never expressed before. With some exploration, it was determined that these difficulties had started following a change in Tina's placement in language arts and math class. After monitoring her performance, the classroom teacher had moved Tina from the standard group to the accelerated group in these areas. Even with some time to adjust, Tina continued to be overwhelmed by the increased pace of instruction. Her symptoms subsided once the parents initiated a change back to the standard group for language arts. She remained in the advanced group for math, a subject she particularly enjoyed, and she became an enthusiastic student again.*

> *A different plan was put into place for a high school junior who also began to show signs of stress. Andre's stress emerged as a change in attitude toward studying and in planning for college. His interest in researching his college options diminished, and he began to shrug off increasingly poor performance at school. Uncharacteristic for their son, Andre's parents shared their concerns with him and expressed an interest in understanding what was going on and what they could do to help. They learned that juggling the demands of school, along with the added pressure of managing the college application process, was overwhelming*

Andre. They offered to help him by enlisting the school guidance counselor to help him lay out the process and timeline for steps in the college application process. Further, they obtained a tutor to help him keep up with his classes and to learn the organizational skills he needed to track all of his demands. With these supports in place, Andre began to feel more in control and competent, and his attitude changed.

If You Need to Change Expectations

If you feel that demands so exceed your child's abilities that she cannot succeed, then you may find yourself going against the current in re-aligning expectations. The current culture, at least here in the United States, seems to be characterized by a more-is-better approach. If reading at age six is good, then reading at age four must be better! If being good at school or athletics or music is an advantage, then doing all three must be even better! There are many factors at work that lead to this general competitive climate for kids (and adults!), and it is far outside the scope of this book to explore these. However, as you consider scaling back your expectations, be forewarned that you may meet with resistance from others in your child's world.

Indeed, we hope it is clear that we are not arguing for coddling kids, setting low expectations, or any of the other ways to describe under-valuing our kids' abilities to rise to a challenge. However, if you have carefully looked for the clues outlined above, including obtaining the opinion of a third party if you are unsure about expectations, and you feel that the bar is set too high, then go ahead and swim against the current!

Your Child's Expectations

Another tricky aspect of setting realistic expectations for kids with executive weaknesses is that they may resist the support they need. Especially for adolescents and young adults, the societal pressure and internal drive to succeed independently are very strong. But the reality is that you can only do as well as you can do. Children with delayed development of executive skills need and deserve external supports and accommodations so they can fairly demonstrate their competencies. Just as we wouldn't expect a child with a physical disability requiring a wheelchair to compete in a foot race with typically-developing peers, we shouldn't ask a child with executive dysfunction to independently manage certain tasks and situations.

We can best support our kids by helping them to understand that the executive functions are brain-based skills and that difficulties with them are <u>not</u> moral or personal weaknesses. You have great ability to understand your child and your child's needs. When you are unsure, consultation with a psychologist or other mental health professional may be useful.

Your Partner's Expectations

Don't be surprised if you and your significant other have divergent views on your child and where to set the bar. One of you wants to back down on expectations, while the other one thinks that providing stronger consequences is in order. This is quite common and may represent a situation in which it makes sense to consult with an objective third party. Last but certainly not least, blaming yourself or your partner as the biological source of these weaknesses is never productive. Feel free to take credit for your daughter's strong intelligence and artistic talent; acknowledge your shared executive weaknesses, if that is the case, but don't spend too much time there. More important is how you all move forward together.

Fading Support

Once you have provided external support for a period of time, it is important to "fade" out supports to see if your child can assume these functions. Fading supports means that you gradually reduce the amount of external support to the point where you are no longer involved at all. For example, perhaps you are working with your child on a daily basis to empty her backpack, sort the papers, and then organize them. To fade support, you might move first from doing the job with your child to observing and cuing as your child does it. The next step might be to back off from cuing, but to ask to see the backpack and notebook after they are organized. Then you might move to reviewing this every other day, then to random checks.

If your child continues to perform the task consistently and does the job relatively well, then you know that she is able to be independent on this task. However, if she falters at any step of the fading process, be prepared to back up to the last level of input at which the child was successful. It is very important to view this as an experiment rather than a "pass-fail" experience. If your child has developed sufficient independent skills, you will not need to keep providing support. However, if your child cannot yet manage, reinstate the structure and guidance until it is again time to "test the waters."

11

Helping Children Control Impulses

> **Impulse control** = The ability to stop and think before acting. Impulse control is also called inhibition. Disinhibited kids are those who lack age-appropriate impulse control.

Often when people talk about a person who is inhibited, they are referring to someone who is constricted or uptight. While this extreme of too much inhibition is generally agreed to be a negative characteristic, a good amount of inhibition *is* critical for behavioral control. The ability to stop and think provides a cushion of time between impulses or feelings and a behavioral response. Thus, impulse control is critical to adaptive self-regulation.

Young children are not expected to consistently control their impulses or their thoughts and actions; they rely heavily on adults to help them control their behavior. They require immediate and concrete guidance. As kids mature, we expect them to internalize rules and to develop better and better self-control so that they are not at the mercy of their impulses. However, not all children develop at the same pace as their peers in this critical arena of executive functioning.

Strategies reviewed in this chapter help children who:
- have trouble controlling verbal impulsiveness (e.g., talking excessively, interrupting others);

- have trouble controlling physical impulsiveness (e.g., grabbing things, pushing and shoving others, hitting);
- have trouble controlling irritating behavior;
- run off in stores or other settings; and
- have problems doing homework.

Below, we've listed general intervention strategies that you'll want to employ with your child or student with impulse control issues. Further down, we've provided advice for dealing with more specific scenarios that you're likely to experience with your child or teen. Note that depending on the issue you are addressing with your child, you will typically use only a subset of the strategies discussed in this chapter.

SUMMARY: GENERAL STRATEGIES TO HELP YOUR CHILD CONTROL IMPULSES

Provide external structure, in the form of general guidelines and specific rules, to teach acceptable behavior.

Offer support (e.g., visual cues, verbal prompts) to bolster the "stop" function.

Plan in advance for potentially problematic times by identifying what leads to loss of control and providing extra support in those situations.

Teach alternatives to negative behaviors. For younger children, teach specific tricks in the form of behaviors that interfere with impulsive physical responses. For older children, work with them to brainstorm more positive responses to the situations.

Build on the older child's desire for more freedom by directly connecting this to the behaviors needed to maturely handle the desired privileges. Align yourself with your child's strong developmental urges, and take a teaching rather than a punishing role. Speak to your child's wishes and use these as a natural spur toward better impulse control.

Use rewards (tangible, verbal, or otherwise) to motivate desired behavior. If rewards alone do not work, you may also need to take away privileges or allow the natural consequence to occur. Be sure to let your child know in advance that he may lose privileges.

Ensure your child's safety. If your child's impulsive behavior puts him at risk of physical harm, drop all other priorities, forget teaching anything, and grab that kid!

Strategies to Help a Child Manage Verbal Impulsiveness (Talking Excessively, Interrupting Others, etc.)

1. Provide external structure by teaching rules that can be applied to a variety of situations. For example:
   - "When you walk into a room, stop and listen to see if the grown-ups are talking. If they are, say, 'Excuse me' then wait for the go-ahead before you jump in."
   - "If you want to join a group of kids who are talking, listen first to what they are talking about, and then you can add a brief comment on that same topic."
   - "Do not talk when the teacher is talking. Raise your hand and wait for the teacher to call on you."

2. Clearly lay out expectations for specific situations so the child knows what is expected. For example:
   - "I need some quiet time now. Please find something quiet that you can do on your own for fifteen minutes."
   - "This is adult talk time. You may stay in the room if you can play quietly without interrupting."
   - "Dad and I have a few things we need to discuss alone. Please find something to do in another room until we have finished."

3. Offer support to bolster the "stop" function. Work out some private cues with your child, so that you can help him know when to stop. For example:
   - Put a finger to your lips or hold up a hand, traffic cop style, to indicate "No talking."
   - Use a visual image to indicate "No Interruption" time in the classroom, such as a laminated picture of a big ear to show this is listening time.
   - When a student interrupts while the teacher is talking, the teacher can raise his hand as a simple and gentle reminder for the student to do the same.
   - In a middle school classroom, the teacher may turn the lights on and off when too many students are talking at the same time. This can also work at home when kids tune out verbal reminders to sit quietly.
   - In high schools, teachers often use physical proximity to cue the student that it is not an appropriate time to talk. The

teacher may walk over to stand near a student's desk, perhaps putting a hand on the student's shoulder. The goal is to be subtle enough to avoid embarrassing the student.

- A parent or a teacher can provide an agreed-upon nonverbal cue to halt talking out of turn.
- Use a verbal prompt to help a child think about the rules, for example:
  - ➤ "What is the rule for entering a room when people may already be talking?"
  - ➤ "Remember, no talking if you are going to stay in the room while I make my phone calls."
- When you see that your child is already about to boil over, support his controls by briefly validating his feelings then reminding him of the rules and possible consequences. "I can see that you're getting really upset. I certainly understand why you're feeling angry, but remember that if you lose control, you will have to take a break in your room. I don't think you would like that much. I know you can hold it together."

J.P. is a sixteen-year-old who lives and breathes football. He gets very upset when a teammate flubs a play, and he routinely responds with strong language and profanities. Although he is a valued player, his behavior has gotten the coach upset enough to suspend him from games. Even his close friends on the team are starting to resent his negative comments. J.P. understands that his behavior is inappropriate, but he has trouble containing his strong reactions in the moment. J.P.'s coach is working with him to develop alternative behaviors. After trying a few different options, J.P. has learned that seeking out visual contact with the coach when he is upset helps him to stay in control. During practice, the coach helps him by calling his name to prompt him when risky situations occur.

4. Plan in advance. When possible, head off problems by setting the scene ahead of time and laying out the guidelines. For example:
   - "After dinner we would like some adult talk time with Grandma and Grandpa. Please think about what you would like to do. You may stay in the room if you can play quietly without interrupting. Or you could do a puzzle in the family room or play with some of your other toys. However, it will be grown-ups only for half an hour after dinner."

- Hand out note cards to students to write down questions or thoughts during uninterrupted lectures.
- Ask talkative kids to think ahead of time of something to do during long drives, waiting during an adult appointment, or other times that are ripe for excessive chatter. Bringing a few books or an MP3 player can make for a more successful outing.
- Encourage kids who come on too strong in social situations to practice laying low. "Laurie, remember that when you go into Jan's house she may have other girls over, too. I know that sometimes you feel left out if others are not including you in their conversation. That's when you might jump in too quickly. You have to think about laying low. Listen first, and then slowly offer some comments on their topic."
- Warn your child in advance when you are going to impose a limit that is likely to spark a verbal outburst. "Okay guys, brace

TRY THIS!

Sometimes we prescribe a pre-arranged short period of whining or complaining for kids. Sound strange? Here's how it works. If you have a child who tends to respond to some commonly occurring event with a verbal outburst, you can set up an opportunity for the child to complain in advance. "Sam, I know that you really don't like it when I tell you that it's time to put your toys away and start on your homework. So, from now on, I'm going to let you know ahead of time, and you will have five minutes to complain. You *must* use that time to complain and I encourage you to use the *full* five minutes so that you really get your feelings out. I will let you know when complaining time is over."

It is important that this be done without condescending to or demeaning the child in any way. It is a real, if humorous, task that teaches children that they *do* have control over their complaining. After all, if they can turn it on and off for a pre-arranged time, then they can control it at other times, too! Don't lecture the child about the purpose of the task. The learning will occur from the experience itself. Generally, over time, the child will become less and less interested in complaining about whatever it is that used to get him started!

yourselves. I'm going to tell you something you're not going to like, but you need to remember that whining, fussing, or screaming is only going to make matters worse for you. Take a deep breath. Here comes the news: We need to leave the park in five minutes."

5. Use rewards to reinforce successful behavior. For example:
   - When a child responds to the guidelines and plays quietly during adult conversation time, respond immediately by offering to play a game or do something of his choosing as soon as the adults are finished talking. If this is a new behavior that you are just starting to work on, do not wait until the end of the adult time. Go over after just a few minutes and whisper to the child that you are very proud of how well he is doing, and encourage him to keep up the good work.
   - For students with a history of calling out in class, reinforce them for raising their hands with a smile and by calling on them.
   - Sometimes, a wink or a thumbs-up is just the right subtle way to reinforce a behavior.
   - For kids who have a really hard time inhibiting the urge to talk, a formal behavioral plan may be necessary. There are many versions of these, but all involve using age-appropriate rewards for the desired behavior (e.g., a sticker for each

TIPS: Remember that spontaneous sharing is one of the joys of human interaction. Differentiate between excessive talking in the form of routine chatter and occasions when something exciting or upsetting has happened.

If a child interrupts, and you say you will be with him in "just a minute," then you need to do just that! Otherwise, you will have no credibility the next time, and the phrase "wait a minute" will rightfully be understood as just a way to put the child off. If it will really be five minutes, then say that. You may need to use a clock or timer to keep yourself honest!

half hour period in the classroom without interruptions, or perhaps coupons toward pizza with the teacher for an older child). We provide more information about behavior modification techniques in Chapter 9.

Strategies to Help a Child Manage Physical Impulsiveness (Grabbing, Pushing and Shoving Others, Hitting, etc.)

1. Provide external structure in the form of general guidelines and specific rules. Teach rules that can be applied in a variety of situations. For example:
   - "David, it is not okay to hurt people. No hitting. Not ever. Unless your life depends on it. If you are angry, there are other ways to handle angry feelings. Let's discuss some options."
   - "Sarah, if someone grabs something from you, you can look them in the eye and say, 'That's mine. Give that back.' But we do not hit other people in this classroom."

2. Clearly lay out expectations for specific situations so the child knows what is expected. For example:
   - "Jack and Susan, you will each have a turn with the new pool toy. I am going to use my watch to keep track of the time. Ten minute turns each. If you grab the toy before it's your turn, then you will lose your next ten minute turn."

3. Teach alternatives to negative behaviors, i.e., replace a negative behavior with a different, possibly unexpected, behavior. For example:
   - A creative teacher of a small class of young children in a therapeutic preschool instructed all of her young students to hold onto their pants legs when they lined up to leave the classroom. This positive directive ("Hold onto your pockets!") engaged the children in a behavior that counteracted the pushing and shoving that so often occurred when the children moved to a different location.
   - A Speech/Language Pathologist in the same program found it difficult to set up her materials at the beginning of group intervention sessions. Seated across from her at a table, the students' little hands darted out to reach for the novel, interesting materials as she took them out of her bag. She devised a simple, very effective approach to helping the children manage

their impulsiveness. Before taking out her materials, she directed the children to hold on to the edge of the table, rewarding them with a sticker on every hand that was holding on.

TRY THIS!

One way to teach alternatives to impulsive physical behaviors is by stopping the action and doing a retake. "Whoa, what's going on here, David? I can see that you are angry, but it is not okay to hit when you are angry. You can say, 'I'm mad' and stomp your foot, but you cannot hit. Let me hear it. Say, 'I'm mad!' Good, now tell me what you are so mad about." Thus, the adults go through a pre-set problem-solving conversation: they identify the feeling triggering David's unacceptable behavior, re-state the rule, provide an alternative, and then require immediate practice. As David starts to use the new behaviors spontaneously, they will encourage him to build a broader repertoire of skills by brainstorming different ways to handle strong feelings.

4. Build on the older child's desire for more freedom by tying the use of proper behavior to an independent activity. For example:
   • "Tonya, I know that you want to rent that karate video game. My concern is that you are already having trouble controlling yourself when your brother irritates you. Show me that you can control your temper with your brother and find other ways to solve your conflicts with him besides physical fighting, and I will reconsider whether you can rent the game. We will talk about this again at the end of the week."

TIP: Impulsive physical responses to frustration must be differentiated from dangerous physical aggression. The latter is quite problematic—whether at home or in a classroom—and will require targeted intervention beyond the scope of this book.

Strategies to Help a Child Stop Irritating Behavior

1. Provide external structure by teaching rules that can be applied to a variety of situations. For example:
   - "It is hard for others to listen to the teacher or get their work done when there are distracting noises. No mouth sounds except for talking at the agreed-upon times when you are in the classroom."
   - "It is rude to grab things off a serving plate. If you would like a cookie, you need to ask for someone to pass the plate. Then you may gently take one."
   - "Pushing in line is not polite. You must wait your turn. When you stand in line, you need to stay in your own space. Do not push against the people ahead of you."

2. Clearly lay out expectations for specific situations so the child knows what is expected. For example:
   - "Rachel, it looks like we will have to wait in line for a little while. I expect you to stand here next to me until it is our turn to order food. No pushing and no running off."
   - "Jack, your brother needs to get his homework done now. No talking to him or crawling around under the table. He needs quiet time and a calm space until he is done."

3. Offer support to bolster the stop function, i.e., work out with the child some private cues, so that you can help him know when to stop. For example:
   - Use simple, nonjudgmental language to cue the child to stop, for example:
     - ➤ "Arthur, tapping your pencil bothers the other kids. You need to stop."
   - Work directly with the child to create an unobtrusive nonverbal signal to cue the need to stop the behavior of concern. For a pencil tapper, perhaps holding up a pencil would do the trick. Or tapping once or twice on the student's desk. Consider this a collaborative, trial-and-error effort between you and the child to figure out what works.
   - Use a verbal prompt to help the child think about the rules, for example:

➤ "Matthew, we are going to pick up your brother from his music lesson. We may have to wait for him to finish. Do you remember the rules during Michael's music lesson? You must stay in the waiting area and not make loud noises."

4. Plan in advance. When possible, head off problems by setting the scene ahead of time and laying out the guidelines. For example:
   - "Sarah, before we leave the car we need to talk about guidelines for when we are in the doctor's office. I know that it is tempting to sing to the music on your MP3 player, but please keep the music in your head and not out loud."
   - "Emma, we are going into the restaurant in just a minute. Remember, when you swing your feet under the table, you end up kicking other people. We will try to give you some extra space by putting you at the end of the table. Please try to keep your feet under your own chair."

5. Teach alternatives to negative behaviors, i.e., replace a negative behavior with a different, possibly unexpected, behavior. For example:
   - "Jared, here is a pipe cleaner for you to hold in your hands while we wait for the show to start. You may not poke your brother or pull on my sweater. Keep your hands busy with the pipe cleaner instead." (Many different quiet, soft toys work well in this regard. Look for "fidget" toys that have some texture or other kinesthetic property of interest. For kids who like to draw, you can teach them to keep a small note pad with them so they have something to do during down time.)

6. Use rewards to reinforce successful behavior. For example:
   - When working with a child to build better control of a specific behavior, it is important to reinforce periods of good control. The more difficult the situation or entrenched the behavior, the more important it is to offer praise or provide concrete rewards.
   - For specific behaviors that recur, a behavioral plan can help the child by reinforcing good control. As noted above, there are many versions of behavioral plans, but all involve using age-appropriate rewards for the desired behavior (e.g., five minutes of free time for each half hour of quiet work). Build in success by using frequent rewards and adjusting the goal to start the child at a level that allows him to meet expectations

a large percentage of the time. You should continue to adjust expectations upward as the child's abilities increase.

TRY THIS!

When we work with families with impulsive children, we often introduce them to the metaphor used by authors Patricia O. Quinn, M.D. and Judith M. Stern, M.A. in their book, *Putting on the Brakes*. Even young children can understand that some kids, like cars, have weak brakes. We explain to the child that he must exercise his brakes to make them stronger and that his parents will help him to do so. It is a metaphor that translates into immediate understanding and lends itself to brief, direct verbal prompts. "Denise, you are moving so fast that you are bumping into people. You need to put on your brakes."

Strategies to Help a Child Control Running Off in Stores or Other Settings

1. Provide external structure by teaching rules that can be applied to a variety of situations. For example:
   - "Jake, when we go for a walk you must always be within my sight. We need to be able to see each other's eyes. It is dangerous for you to run off where I cannot see you."
   - "Sally, in a crowded place, it is easy for me to lose track of you or for you to lose track of me. So in crowded places, you must stay right with me. 'Right with me' means that you are within one arm's length. Let's practice that so that I am sure you understand what it means."
   - "Ted, you must always ask for permission before you leave the classroom to get a drink from the water fountain or for any other reason. I must know where you are at all times."

2. Clearly lay out expectations for specific situations so the child knows what is expected. For example:
   - "Jake, this is just a quick trip into the grocery store. We need just three things, and we need to get done as quickly as possible so we can make it to the post office before they close. You

TRY THIS!

Set up scenarios with your child to role play desired behaviors. For example, children who are impulsive may not think of their own behavior in a store as "running off," but rather as "just looking at something." So, set up the scene at home where one of you is picking out groceries and the other goes to look at something down at the end of the aisle. Can you both still see each other? What about if one of you goes around the corner? What if a couple of people come into that aisle and block your view? What should you do then? Work out what is acceptable and what is not. Giving your child the opportunity to play the role of the adult, sometimes, may enhance learning (and fun!). Then, the next time you are in the real-life situation, offer praise when your child shows you that he has learned from your role playing.

must stick right with me. In and out in ten minutes. Stay right next to me; we're moving fast. Do you think we can do it?"

- "Andrew, I know you like to ride ahead a bit when we go bike riding. But we have to cross a busy street here to get to the bike trail. We will walk our bikes over to the bike trail together. Stay right with me until I say that it is safe to get back on your bike and ride ahead. Okay, now right next to me for this part."

- "Brianna, it looks like the kids are all playing outside. The Smiths have a big backyard, and you kids can have fun playing there. But you may not leave the backyard, even if some of the bigger kids go down to the creek. You must stay in the backyard and come talk to me first if you want to go anywhere else. I will be right here on the patio or inside in the kitchen."

3. Offer support to bolster the stop function, i.e., work out with the child some private cues, so that you can help him know when to stop. For example:
   - Ted's teacher has taped a large red stop sign to the inside of the door to remind him of the rule to ask permission before leaving the classroom. He prompts Ted verbally, if needed. ("Stop at the stop sign, Ted.")

- When they go to the mall, if Sally starts to drift too far away, her mother gives her a simple reminder. ("Sally, arm's length please.")
- Sarah's field trip group leader prompts her verbally before they get off the bus. "Sarah, we are getting off the bus soon to enter the museum. Do you remember the important field trip rule we talked about earlier? What was that rule?"

4. Plan in advance. When possible, head off problems by setting the scene ahead of time and laying out the guidelines. For example:
   - "William, we are going into the grocery store in just a minute. Remember the grocery store rules: You stay right with the cart and me, and only the things I say go into the cart. If you do not stay near me, then you will need to sit in the cart while we shop. Now, you tell me the store rules before we go inside."
   - "I know that you and your friends prefer to sit together without a grown-up in the movie theater. I will let you girls sit alone, and I will sit in the back of the theater. If you go to the bathroom or to buy snacks, you must go with at least one other person. I will lay low until the movie is over unless I see you getting too wild or not following the rules."
   - "Sarah, I know how excited you get when the class goes on a field trip, and that you get so interested in things that you just can't wait to see them all. But this is very important: You must stay with your group leader at all times. No exceptions. If you want to look at something in the museum, you must wait until the group moves on together. If you or one of the other girls needs to use the bathroom, you must tell your group leader and you will all go together. Okay? I want to make sure that you understand the rules of the day. You stay with the group leader. No exceptions."

5. Teach alternatives to negative behaviors, i.e., replace a negative behavior with a different, possibly unexpected, behavior. For example:
   - A creative preschool teacher working with a small group of impulsive children was faced with the task of keeping them all together, even the ones who had a history of running off. She fashioned a long rope with four loops on it. Whenever they went anywhere as a group (e.g., down the hall or out to the van), each child was instructed to hold onto his loop.

- In the grocery store, parents often find that keeping kids involved prevents boredom and the accompanying tendency to wander off. "Jake, I need your help to get everything on my list. Right now I need carrots. Can you go get one bag of carrots for me? Put them in the basket and then I will tell you what to get next."

- "Alex, the class is going to the bus now. I need a helper to count off as each person heads out the door. Would you please stand next to me at the door and be my head counter? Then you can be my partner as we go to the bus."

6. Use rewards to reinforce successful behavior. For example:
   - "Jake, you are doing a great job following the grocery store rules. Keep up the good work." (verbal praise)
   - "Ashley, there is a sticker waiting for you when we get on the bus if you follow all the rules for lining up and leaving the building. Remember those rules? Stay with your partner and stay behind the buddies in front of you in line."

7. Ensure your child's safety by using hands-on tactics. For example:
   - Running off is simply too risky a behavior in some situations. If the situation is dangerous, then you just need to deal with the behavior by ensuring that it will not happen. That is why we hold small children by the hand in a parking lot. However, with impulsive children, the hands-on approach is often necessary in other situations, as well.
   - Sammy's mom often endured the disapproving looks of other shoppers when she took her young son to the mall. Knowing that he would run off to explore things he found interesting, she used a children's safety harness/leash that she attached to the back of his overalls. In fact, she was always careful to dress Sammy in overalls for risky outings so that she would have a way to attach what she called her umbilical line. Ensuring her son's safety and her own peace of mind always outweighs her desire to blend in with the other parents at the mall.
   - Amanda had no fear of the water, even though she could not swim! Whether or not she had her "floaties" on, Amanda would run off and jump in the water. Amanda's parents developed a no-exceptions policy when near the pool. They put

her floaties on her before she left the car to enter the swim club. If she took them off at any time they were at the pool, they immediately packed up their things and took her home for the rest of the day.

TIP: When you impose a consequence in response to your child's behavior, let the consequence do most of the teaching rather than over-talking the issues or getting into an argument. A simple re-statement of the rule and the consequences, followed by action, is what is needed. "Amanda, you are not allowed to take off your floaties when we are at the pool because it is too dangerous. We will need to go home now." Your child may get upset and argue about the consequences or promise to do better the rest of the day. ("I won't do it again! I promise! I'll be really, really good!") As difficult as it can be (particularly if it is a nice day and you want to stay at the pool!), your child will learn best if you follow-through with a minimum of words and emotion. "Sorry, Amanda. You didn't follow the rule. You will have another chance tomorrow." Experiencing the consequences for the problematic behavior is the source of the learning.

Strategies to Help a Child Manage Homework Problems

1. Provide external structure by teaching rules that can be applied to a variety of situations. For example:

- "Drew, during homework time your computer is only to be used for school work. I know how tempting it is to instant message your friends. But you lose a lot of time when you jump into conversations online. So, before starting your homework, you must close the instant messaging program."
- "Sarah, homework comes before electronics and telephone time. You can take some time to unwind a bit when you get home. Have a snack and hang out for awhile. However, you must finish your homework before you get the other privileges."

- "Alex, after band practice you need to come home so you can get your homework done. No last minute decisions to go somewhere with your friends. You must come right home after practice."
- "Jen, getting enough sleep to be well-rested is important for all of us. All of your homework needs to be done early enough in the evening to have time to settle down for bed. So, homework must be done either in the afternoon or right after dinner. We'll see which one works best. What would you like to try first?"
- Or, for a teen: "Allie, I am happy to help you with your homework when you need it, but I really need my sleep to be able to function well the next day. So, any input you want from me has to happen before nine o'clock. I think you do your best work before then, anyway, and you really need to wind down before bed. But if you choose to do your homework later, then you're on your own."
- "Ed, I know how frustrated you get with homework. But it is not okay to treat others badly because of your frustration. When you get upset, you need to take a short break to get yourself under control."

2. Offer support to bolster the "stop" (or in this case, the "review") function by working out with the child some private cues, so that you can help him review work. For example:
   - When Jim finishes work quickly and turns it in ahead of most of the others in his class, Jim's teacher prompts him to review the directions and make sure all questions have been answered. His teacher also reminds him to proofread his answers and lets him step into the hall so he can read his work aloud.
   - Ed's mother often previews his homework with him and encourages him to monitor his frustration level as he works. "That looks like some tough work, because I know that writing can be hard for you. Remember, take a break if you feel yourself getting all worked up inside."

3. Plan in advance. When possible, head off problems by setting the scene ahead of time and laying out the guidelines. For example:
   - "Saundra, today you have a dentist's appointment after school. That means that you must come straight home after school. No stopping at Sheila's house on the way home and no hang-

ing out at the bus stop talking to friends. I expect you to be home by 2:35 p.m."

4. Teach alternatives to negative behaviors, i.e., replace a negative behavior with a different, possibly unexpected, behavior. For example:

- Melanie often rushes through her work and does not read the directions thoroughly. So, Melanie's dad took her to the store and allowed her to choose her own brightly-colored highlighting marker. Now when she sits down to do an assignment, she is required to first highlight the most important words in the directions. Before starting the actual assignment, her parents review the highlighting to be certain she has done that task thoughtfully and has chosen the key words or phrases.
- Melanie was also taught to circle or highlight the operational sign before starting a math calculation problem.
- Jonas makes many careless errors on tests because he jumps in and starts writing before even reading the whole test question. Jonas' teacher now begins each test by asking students to read each question and underline key words (e.g., *not, all, except*).
- Cassie often asks her mother for help with homework, but then gets irritable and rejects her mother's input. Cassie's mom has introduced the concept of "frustration breaks," brief times to step away from the homework and cool down. "Cassie, you're getting really frustrated. Take a few minutes and I'll wait for you here."

5. Use rewards to reinforce successful behaviors. For example:

- Melanie's new behaviors (slowing down and reading directions all the way through) are rewarded in the following manner. If she completes the items on a   page according to the directions, then she is allowed to skip the last one or two problems, depending on the length of the assignment. (Of course, this plan had to be pre-approved by the teacher.)
- When Jim independently and accurately underlines key words on his homework assignments, he earns points toward special privileges. He can trade in his points for weekend privileges (e.g., a trip to the mall) or save them for longer-term rewards (e.g., a day at the water park).

TIPS: Reward systems should be created with the child or teen's input. If the child or teen has selected the possible rewards (with your approval, of course), then he will be a lot more motivated to work toward those goals. In fact, if he also participates in creating the target behaviors that will be rewarded, there is an even greater likelihood of success!

If the reward system that you create is not working well, you might benefit from a more systematic approach to your plan. Seek the guidance of a psychologist or behavior specialist, whether indirectly through reading up on reward systems (see the book on raising defiant children by Russell Barkley in our reference list), or if you need more direct help, by seeking a professional consultation.

CASE STUDY: PUTTING IT ALL TOGETHER

Trevor is a young boy who often interrupts his parents' conversations. A bright, verbal, and exuberant child, he both charms and irritates people with his constant stream of chatter.

Now, when Trevor comes bursting into a room, talking as he enters, Trevor's parents remind him to stop and listen to see if others are talking. They have taught him these rules: listen first, say "Excuse me" if others are talking and he wants to say something, then wait for the go-ahead. They still need to provide reminders, sometimes several times a day. ("Trevor, did you listen as you came into the kitchen?") Sometimes, they just put a finger to their lips to quiet him. When Trevor's excessive talking gets to be too much, they request quiet time. ("Trevor, my listener is feeling full right now. I need some quiet time for a few minutes. Please find something quiet to do on your own.")

When possible, Trevor's parents warn him ahead of time if they know they will need some adults-only conversation time. They help him to think ahead and to plan some things to do while the adults are talking.

Trevor's parents are very conscious of providing frequent feedback, praising him for controlling his talking. Trevor has been begging to have a sleep-over with a friend in a tent in the backyard. He and his parents have worked out a system wherein Trevor's self-control earns him points toward this goal.

Transitioning from Short-Term to Long-Term Goals

For children who struggle with impulse control, the goal is for them to learn ways to interject a brief moment of thought before acting. This time allows for more accurate interpretation of events. ("Maybe he didn't mean to push me. Maybe he just got jostled by all these kids in the hallway.") It also allows for consideration of consequences. ("Jack is a nice guy. I could really mess things up if we get into a shoving match when he really didn't mean to do it.")

Remember that better behavioral control comes about as the result of both learning and brain development. This means that the younger your child and the more impulsive he is, the longer the trajectory will likely be for developing control. There is no quick fix here.

We start teaching better impulse control by providing clear guidelines for behavior. This external structure provides the model for the internal structure we want the child to eventually develop. Short-term goals include ensuring the child's safety, preventing a loss of behavioral control (and negative social-emotional consequences), and allowing the child to engage in experiences necessary for healthy development. Following the general principles for behavior modification, we use concrete reinforcers and frequent verbal praise for following the rules and putting on the brakes. We use reasonable consequences for serious lapses in behavior. Ultimately, we are trying to move our children toward internalized controls, but this is done step by step.

When a child responds impulsively, use the incident to reinforce expectations and to offer suggestions about better ways to handle the situation. In this way, the child begins to build a repertoire of behaviors that will serve him in the long run. Once your child begins to show evidence of even rudimentary self-control, then you can best support this growth by verbal or concrete reinforcement. The amount of self-control is not fixed; children's behavior will vary from one setting to another. Prompt the child with verbal or physical cues.

You are working towards fading out the prompting, and this should happen in tandem with your observations of your child's development. What eventually replaces your prompting? It is a sort of internal dialogue that we may be aware of, at times, even as adults. The voice that we hear as we are on the edge of yelling at our spouse or the person with a cartload of groceries in the express checkout lane tells us that behaving badly will not help the situation. Sometimes, we even hear the voice of our parent or other teacher. So, consider this your reminder to choose your words carefully when you teach your children. What words and what tone of voice do you want them to hear in their heads when they think of you?

Educate Others and Advocate For Your Child

As you educate yourself about your child's behavior and the role of the executive functions, you will surely notice that you understand and handle your child's impulsive behavior differently than you did before. Providing information to other adults in your child's life, too, will promote sensitive handling of his executive weaknesses in the varieties of settings in which he operates.

This can be done informally, such as in conversation with the babysitter when she complains that she had to tell Johnny three times in one day to use words rather than his hands when he was upset. Or, it can be done in a more systematic manner, such as by giving others articles to read (or lending them this book).

Working with impulsive children can be very frustrating as they tend to repeat the same behaviors over and over in spite of knowing what they "should" do. They may also demonstrate great variability (inconsistency) in their behavior, depending on the day and situation. The inconsistency in the behavior can lead others to mistakenly assume that it is a lack of motivation that causes the problem. "He did well yesterday, but today he chose to ignore the rules." It is important for adults to remember that the behavior of impulsive children occurs in the moment. By definition, they do not think before they act.

Talk to your child's teacher about his issues, and get a feel for how the behavior is being handled in that setting. Just as important as how the teacher handles lapses in control is what is being done to support and teach better self-control. In many cases, you will want to ask for a meeting with all the school staff dealing with your child.

Conveying your understanding of impulsiveness and what to do about it can be the lead-in to a cooperative relationship based upon the shared concern of all involved with your child's well-being. As we have hopefully made clear, we do not mean to suggest that understanding your child means giving him a free pass on meeting behavioral expectations. It is sensitive and informed handling that we are working toward.

Final Thoughts

Although it is tempting to lecture kids, this is not effective if the primary weakness is impulse control. Instead, stay focused on the specific behavior, apply the principles of intervention, and try to stick to a straightforward, nonjudgmental, problem-solving approach. And know that you will repeat yourself often, because developing self-control requires practice and maturation over time.

Perhaps your child is not the only one working to develop self-control. Do you find yourself yelling whenever your child has lapses in control? Do you physically grab your child when the child does something impulsive? Then you, too, must learn better control. It is important to remember that much of your child's irritating or impulsive behavior is not intentional. Prepare yourself in advance of difficult situations by setting your own intentions. Think of a few key words to keep yourself calm and plan your own internal response for impulsive behavior. ("Keep your cool." "Terry is impulsive because it is his nature, not because he intends to do it." "Don't lecture him; just tell him what he needs to do." "Stop and take a calming break for both of us if we need it.")

Don't neglect your own needs. As the parent of a child with executive dysfunction and someone perhaps struggling with it yourself, you need to seek out support, even if all you can manage is a cup of coffee or a phone call with a sympathetic friend. If your own behavior in response to your child continues to be out of control, and practice does not help you to build a more thoughtful, systematic approach, then you may need the help of a mental health professional to learn these parenting skills.

12

Helping Children Shift Gears

Cognitive Flexibility = The ability to think and problem-solve in a flexible, dynamic manner. This includes the ability to adapt to changes and to flexibly generate a variety of ways to view a situation or solve a problem.

Even with a well-established routine, life at home, at school, and with peers is filled with changes and unexpected events. Children who are rigid in their view of the world have great difficulty adapting to change and generating new ways to solve problems. They cling to familiar approaches and routines. They may also have trouble learning from experiences and recognizing similarities between situations and tasks.

Cognitively rigid children may be critical of others, as these children expect absolute adherence to the rules. As with other areas of executive functioning, a child may be very intelligent and still lack cognitive flexibility.

Strategies in this chapter help children who:

- have difficulty with transitions;
- have difficulty adapting to new situations or environments;
- become upset when their peers "break the rules" or behave in unexpected ways; and

- are frustrated when their first attempt to solve a problem isn't successful.

Below, we've listed general intervention strategies that you'll want to employ with your child or student who has trouble being flexible. Further down, we've provided advice for dealing with more specific scenarios that you're likely to experience with your child or teen. Note that depending on the issue you are addressing with your child, you will typically use only a subset of the strategies discussed in this chapter.

SUMMARY: GENERAL STRATEGIES TO HELP YOUR CHILD SHIFT GEARS

Create a consistent, predictable environment as much as possible.

Create visual cues for routines and schedules.

Highlight changes to the routine and help the child build a bridge from the familiar to the unfamiliar.

Provide additional support during transitions and when new concepts, tasks, or environments are introduced.

Allow additional time to adjust to changes in routine.

Teach the child to walk through new situations and changes. This includes teaching self-talk (e.g., "this is different but that doesn't mean it is bad," "I need to figure out the best thing to do even though this is new") as well as determining when to seek external assistance.

Model multiple ways of approaching a task or situation. When you are faced with one of the many changes in routine (both expected and unexpected) that occur in your life, model a flexible approach for your child. Talk it through aloud, narrating your thinking.

Provide a place for self-calming during stressful times and teach self-soothing techniques.

Strategies to Help Reduce a Child's Difficulty with Transitions

1. Create a consistent, predictable environment to the extent possible. Try to build in continuity from one day to the next, even in

the midst of change, and minimize the number of "exceptions" to the general schedule. For example:

- David's mom started his school year with a daycare arrangement that she thought would work well. The daycare was run out of a private home and was able to accommodate her unpredictable shift changes at work and allowed her to send David or not each day just by placing a call to the daycare mom. After a difficult few weeks that clearly challenged her son's flexibility beyond his ability to adapt, she set up a new plan that involved providing after-school care for him and two other neighborhood children in her own home. By sharing the expense, she could afford to have David in a situation that allowed him to come home to his own house every day.

- Rachel's divorced parents have an amicable relationship, and they are able to accommodate one another's schedule preferences from week to week. However, their daughter has demonstrated that she is not able to handle these changes well. They now keep a very systematic, predictable schedule so that she knows exactly what days and times she will be with each parent. While there are changes, of course, for various unavoidable events or for vacations, they are generally able to adhere to a consistent schedule.

- Sam's school team has arranged for pull-out services that occur at natural transitions in the school day rather than pulling him from an ongoing activity or returning him to the classroom in the middle of instruction.

- Whenever possible, Matthew's mother schedules doctor's appointments for the beginning or end of the school day, so that he does not need to deal with both leaving and returning to school mid-activity.

2. Create visual cues for routines and schedules, i.e., post daily and long-term schedules. For example:

- Post a daily schedule. This is generally done in classrooms, particularly in the early grades. A daily schedule, perhaps less detailed, can be helpful at home, as well. Use drawings or cut out pictures to create a schedule for nonreaders. For example, draw a picture of a clock showing the times that events will occur. Pair it with a picture representing the event (e.g., pictures of clothing to symbolize getting dressed and a picture of a school bus to symbolize time to be at the bus stop).

- Provide your child with a calendar to use to keep track of the larger picture.
  - ➤ Let your child select a calendar in a favorite theme as a holiday present at the end of the year. For younger children, the adults can set it up by filling in important events. Older children and adolescents can fill it out on their own, with a bit of help.
  - ➤ Include vacations and sports events, and add doctor's appointments and birthday parties as they arise. If you are separated from your child's other parent, and the child is scheduled to visit the other parent, or she travels from one home to another on a visitation schedule, be sure to include words or pictures to indicate "Mom days" and "Dad days."
  - ➤ Teach your child to use the calendar. When your child asks about upcoming events, refer to the calendar. If the child is too young to use the calendar without help, build in an evening ritual that consists of crossing off each day and then looking ahead to the next day or the weekend.
- For younger children especially, who have difficulty making typical transitions throughout their day and in the classroom, commercially available devices like the Time Timer® or the Time Tracker® Visual Timer & Clock can serve to communicate the concept of elapsed time with an easy-to-understand graphic depiction of time remaining. Making the passage of time concrete, a tool like this can help students *see* how much time they have before free play time is over and silent reading begins.

TIP: When you set up calendars or schedules for your child or teen, involve them as much as possible in the process. Many kids enjoy picking out their own calendar, and older children and teens can certainly use the computer to create schedules or calendars. A younger child may enjoy decorating a calendar that you create, either on the computer or by hand. Involvement in the process promotes a sense of ownership, so that the child is more likely to turn to the tool when it is needed. This also teaches skills that will be useful as children and teens begin to independently manage their time.

3. Highlight changes to the routine, i.e., let children know about changes to expected routines in advance. For example:
   - Trial and error helps a child or adolescent learn how much time is needed to prepare for changes. The general guideline of "not too far in advance but not at the last minute" has to be customized for the age and temperament of each child.
   - Be very explicit about highlighting what will be the same and what will be different. "Look at the calendar with me, Katrina. You see you will still visit Daddy on these three Tuesdays, but on *this* Tuesday, Daddy will be out of town for work. Let's cross off the word 'Daddy' from that day and add it here to Friday. Daddy will be home then and you will visit him that week on Friday."

4. Provide additional support during transitions. For example:
   - Assign a peer buddy for transition times.
   - Assign a job to focus the child during transitions (e.g., carrying the volleyballs outside, turning off lights and closing the door to the classroom).
   - Stay near the child during transition times.
   - Preview the transition and then provide verbal support through the process. ("Sarah, we are going to be leaving soon to head home. When it is time to go, you will need to clean up the toys, get your coat on, and say good-bye to your cousins. Got that? Okay, time to start cleaning up.")
   - Provide advance warning to allow the child to prepare for upcoming transitions. ("Adam, you will need to clean up in ten minutes." Let the child know when he is at the five-minute and then the one-minute mark.)

Strategies to Help a Child Adapt to New Situations or Environments

1. Highlight changes and help the child bridge from the familiar to the unfamiliar. For example:
   - "You have a different teacher and a new classroom this year. But your new classroom is in the same wing of the school as your classroom last year, and you will use the same entrance."
   - "Abby, this is a new doctor, but her job is to help us just like Dr. Smith did. She will talk to us about how things are going

at home and at school, and she will help us if we are having any problems."

- "Matt, my work schedule is changing and I will need to stay late on Thursdays. That means that I will not be home for dinner. Dad will get home early so that he can be there when you get off the bus. That way, you can stick to the same after-school schedule that you already know. By the time you eat dinner, do the dishes, and start on your homework, I will be home."

2. Provide additional support, i.e., provide something or someone who is familiar when the child is faced with a situation that will be unfamiliar. For example:
   - Have a parent or other trusted adult accompany the child and walk through the new environment.
   - Assign a familiar peer buddy.
   - Young children often carry a favorite "snuggly" or familiar toy. These are sometimes referred to as transitional objects, and they help a child to master the transition from the familiar to the unfamiliar. Sometimes older children benefit from the same, although the transitional object needs to be something that does not set her up for ridicule by peers. For one girl, a photo of her mother that she kept in her pocket provided the extra measure of security that she needed. Another pre-teen carried in her pocket a small piece of material cut from her childhood blanket. It was the textural feel of the material that soothed her.

3. Preview the situation and be very explicit about what will happen whenever possible. For example:
   - "Jack, your new teacher may ask you to do things differently than Mrs. Miller did. Your job is to follow your new teacher's directions and to ask her if you are unsure or confused about what she wants you to do."
   - "Annisha, when we get to the party, there will be a lot of people. We will know some of them and we will not know a lot of them. The first thing we are going to do is find the table with the cards that tell us where we will be sitting. I know that we will be sitting with Aunt Liz and your cousins, but we will need to find out the table number when we get there."
   - Using puppets, superheroes, stuffed animals, or other toys, set up the scene and play out what will happen. (In fact, if you

observe your child's imaginary play, you may notice how often your child already rehearses life situations through the use of play. Sometimes play is the child's work!)

- Many children, and certainly most teens, are uncomfortable with imaginary play with toys. Try role-playing instead. If you have a video camera, you can make a video together of the scenario, how you expect things to go, and what each person will likely be doing. For highly sensitive or anxious kids, reverse roles so that they play the adult role and you are the child dealing with the new situation or change.
- Expect and accept that the child will likely feel stressed by changes. Don't try to talk the child out of her feelings nor treat them as forces that need to be cast out. Acknowledge the feelings, provide verbal support and encouragement, and soldier on.

4. Allow additional time to adjust to new situations, i.e., set up a "dry run" in advance to familiarize the child with the situation, if possible. For example:
   - Ask the school to schedule a visit with the new teacher and classroom a few days before the start of the new school year, if this is not already done routinely. For some children, this is included as an accommodation on the child's education plan or in the formal meeting notes.
   - Take the child to play on the playground of a new school ahead of time, just to build some comfort and familiarity.
   - Visit with a new tutor or daycare provider for a short time a day or two in advance of when the services start.
   - Take a child to observe a karate class or other activity before the child starts lessons.
   - As much as possible, try to keep the routine stable when the child is in the midst of major changes, like getting braces or transitioning to a new school.

5. Try to teach the child to walk through new situations and changes. This includes teaching self-talk (e.g., "This is different but that doesn't mean it is bad" or "I need to figure out the best thing to do even though this is new") as well as determining when to seek assistance. Teach the child to identify her own characteristics in a straightforward, nonjudgmental manner. For example:

- "Denise, this is one of those times where your distaste for change might get in the way. These changes just take a long time for you to get used to, don't they?"
- "Anthony, it looks to me like you have your 'new situations jitters.'"
- "Sally, you have never been to sleep-away camp before. Of course, it will take a little while for you to feel comfortable there. But those are your 'new place blues' kicking in. I think you will have a great time once you settle in. You know you can always call me if you need to talk."

6. Model multiple ways of approaching a task or situation. When you are faced with one of the many changes in routine (both expected and unexpected) that occur in your life, model a flexible approach for your child. Talk it through aloud, narrating your thinking.
   - "I am a little nervous about starting my new job. I think I'll see if I can go in sometime this week at lunch to meet my co-workers and find out a little more about what to expect. It would be helpful to know where my desk will be and where the bathroom is in advance!"
   - "Dad and I are going to a party at the new neighbor's house this evening. I'm not a big fan of large, loud parties so I hope they don't have the whole neighborhood over! I guess if it's a large group I could just find one person I know and talk to that person. It's supposed to be really nice weather, so I could also just sit outside on the deck and enjoy the warm night air while I check out what's happening."

7. Help your child learn strategies to manage the situation and initiate her own coping skills. For example:
   - "Ella, I know that vacations start off being hard for you because of all the new things. But after a day or two, you usually feel better. Let's brainstorm about things we can do to help those first few days go more smoothly."
   - "Chris, I know that you are used to my being at home when you come home after school. Now, it will be Dad who is here on Thursdays instead of me. What would help you to feel more comfortable with this? You can call me on my cell phone when you first get home, if you feel like it."

- "Ashley, you have an overnight band trip coming up. Do you think this is one of those times when you would like me to go along as a chaperone? Or is there someone else that will be going that you could count on for help if you need it?"
- "Jack, birthday parties are exciting, but they also mean that you will be going to a house that you have not been to before. I've spoken to Mike's mom and he will be going to the party, too. How about if I offer to drive Mike so you will have a friend that you know when you walk in. I'll stay at the party, too, for a little while."

8. Help the child understand how the discomfort can affect overall behavior and mood. For example:
   - "Jackie, you are really grumpy today. Sometimes that happens when people are worried about something. I know how hard changes are for you. Do you think that you are worried about going on vacation?"
   - "I know that you have had trouble falling asleep the past few days. I think you might be a little worried about the start of the school year. What do you think?"

TIP: Whether or not your child acknowledges that she's feeling uncomfortable with change, you should still provide a perspective that may allow for better self-awareness in the future. But don't belabor the point with your child. She does not need to acknowledge her feelings in words to benefit from your point.

Strategies to Help a Child Who Becomes Upset when Peers Break the Rules or Behave in Unexpected Ways

1. Provide additional support, verbally. For example:
   - "Chris, Kate is drawing her picture the way that she wants to. And you can draw yours the way that you want to. Both pictures show what spring is like, but you seem to be thinking about different aspects of spring. They are both just fine."

- "Do you remember that I said that kids can sit wherever they like? So, Jack decided that he wanted to sit in a different seat today, and he chose the one that you usually choose. Now it is your turn to pick a different seat. Perhaps this one, right at the same table?"

2. Teach the child to walk through new situations and changes. This includes teaching self-talk (e.g., "This is different but that doesn't mean it is bad," or "I need to figure out the best thing to do even though this is new") as well as determining when to seek external assistance. Teach the child to identify her own characteristics in a straightforward, nonjudgmental manner. For example:
   - Teach specific guidelines, such as: "It is not my job to tell the other kids how to behave. That is a teacher's job." "I'm only in charge of me."
   - For a younger child, ask her to draw a picture of what the new situation may look like. Remind her that the drawing can be changed after she sees what actually happens.
   - "Ada, when you get to camp, there will be all kinds of kids there. Some of them will do things differently than you are used to. That is probably going to make you uncomfortable, because it is hard for you when people do things that you are not used to. As long as they are not hurting you or anyone else, you probably do not need to get involved. But if you are unsure of what to do at any time while you're at camp, what do you think you could do? Is there someone you could ask to help you? I'm thinking that your counselor would be a good 'go-to person.'"

3. Provide a place for self-calming during stressful times and teach self-soothing techniques. Once a child has a meltdown, as so often happens with these issues, it is important to help the child return to a calmer state before even talking about the issues. For example:
   - Teach self-soothing techniques, such as counting to ten or deep breathing. Self-soothing refers to the child's ability to calm herself down when she starts to get anxious or upset. The teaching part generally starts with either modeling a technique when the child is not upset or by doing it with the child once the child needs calming. ("Let's breathe together. Big, deep breaths now. In through your nose and out through your mouth.")

- Many children need to get physical distance from a stressful situation, and they respond best when you've agreed in advance on a special place where they can take a break when they feel out of control. (This is NOT a time-out or a punishment, and adults must be cautious to guard against lapsing into a punishment framework.) For young children, this is often a small, contained space such as the child-sized fabric tunnels available as playthings or a bean bag chair. In one classroom, the teacher provided a small tent, and the child added a few favorite books.
- Be clear and direct, but gentle, with a child when she is overwrought. "Your feeling brain has taken over and you need to quiet your body so you can hear your thinking brain again." Your calm authoritative tone sets the stage, whereas a stressed-out and overly emotional response will escalate the situation.
- Trial-and-error will teach you whether or not the child needs larger personal space once she's upset. Many children having a meltdown respond somewhat like a cornered animal when someone gets too close to them. This is when they often strike out at a parent or teacher. Unless the child or those around her is in physical danger from her actions, give the child space and allow her to take the lead in re-joining you once she feels calm.

Strategies to Help Reduce a Child's Frustration When Her First Attempt to Solve a Problem Isn't Successful

1. Provide additional support verbally. For example:
   - "These problems are really frustrating, aren't they? Try to slow down and let's see where you got off-track."
   - "If you already knew how to do everything, then you wouldn't need to be in school. This one is a hard one. It may take a few tries to figure it out."
   - "Jamie, it looks like the part of you that wants things to be easy is fighting with the part of you that knows what it takes to learn new things. Try to hold on to that new learning mindset here."

2. Teach the child to walk through new situations and changes. This includes teaching self-talk (e.g., "This is different but that doesn't mean it is bad," or "I need to figure out the best thing to do even

though this is new") as well as determining when to seek external assistance. Teach the child to identify her own characteristics in a straightforward, nonjudgmental manner.

- "Emily, you are having trouble with the homework. Remember, when you are feeling frustrated with a task, you need to remind yourself that this is all about learning. It is hard, but it is not impossible."
- "Justin, you are getting a bit irritable with me over this homework. What do you need to do to get back into the right frame of mind? Do you think you need help with the work now or time to calm down?"

3. Provide a place for self-calming during stressful times and teach self-soothing techniques. As noted above, be clear and direct, but gentle, with a child when she is overwrought.

- "It looks like you are getting really frustrated with this writing prompt. Maybe you need a brief break to get your thoughts together. Would you rather hang out in your room or play with the dog?"
- "Alan, you are losing it. Time to calm yourself down. How about taking fifteen minutes, maybe listen to music or go sit on the deck?"
- "Lana, remember how you learned to pull inside your shell like a turtle to give yourself a mental break? I think it's turtle time."
- "Jack, maybe this is the time to use what you learned from the school psychologist. Use your imagination to take yourself to

TRY THIS!

We have found it very helpful to teach kids that strong emotion can interfere with thinking. Let your child know that different parts of the brain are responsible for feelings and problem-solving. Teach her that strong feelings lead to temporary changes in our brains and throughout our bodies. When that occurs, we may not be able to think as clearly as we need to in order to solve problems. To get back to our "thinking brains," we first need to calm ourselves. A framework for understating her emotions will provide your child the perspective she needs to be successful.

CASE STUDY: PUTTING IT ALL TOGETHER

Joanne is a seven-year-old who tends to lose control when her normal routines are interrupted. When plans change, she becomes agitated and often defiant, unable to relinquish her expectations. Both at home and at school, Joanne is thrown by any change in routine. For example, if the cafeteria runs out of the pizza that she eagerly anticipates on Fridays, she may cry and refuse to eat anything else. She is likely to be irritable for the rest of the day. Having a substitute teacher is very hard for her, even one she has met before, because the substitute does not do things exactly the same way that the regular teacher does. Although Joanne enjoys playing with other kids, her cognitive inflexibility makes it hard for her and for them. For example, she has difficulty switching gears when a peer suggests playing outside rather than completing their board game. Vacations are hard on the family, because Joanne really prefers to stay within her familiar surroundings. The rest of her family enjoys going to new places and trying new activities and restaurants, but Joanne balks at the changes in routine.

Like many children with cognitive rigidity, Joanne is thrown by changes and unexpected events. When feasible, her parents review the daily schedule and point out possible changes or other times when she may be at-risk for becoming overwhelmed. They also plan ahead to help her manage changes that have proved problematic in the past. Her parents and teacher have discussed with Joanne the possibility (yes, it might happen again!) that there will be no pizza on Pizza Friday or that they may run out of other menu items on other days. Joanne's parents have provided several canned and microwavable meals that Joanne likes, and the teacher has agreed to keep these in reserve to use as needed. Using dolls to act out the scenario, Joanne and her mother have practiced ways to handle the initial upset feelings that occur when she finds out that there is no more pizza. During play dates at her house, her parents remind her that her guest gets to decide what they play. If she follows that rule, they build in an hour of play time once her friend leaves during which Joanne can decide what she and her mother do. When she is at another kid's house (particularly one she doesn't know very well),

(continued on next page)

(continued from previous page)

her parents may first talk to the other parent(s) to share that she needs some extra time to move from one activity to another and to request that the parent stay somewhat close by in case she needs a bit of support.

Joanne's parents use their own disappointments to model cognitive flexibility. Recently, the family had to forego a planned weekend visit to a friend's beach house because their friend got a nasty case of the flu. They were all disappointed, and they talked together about their feelings, when they could reschedule the visit, and what they could do to make the weekend fun in other ways.

Joanne has benefited from instruction that teaches her that there are rules and exceptions. Rules apply most of the time while exceptions apply some of the time. She does best when a trusted adult or peer helps her manage the exceptions to the rules. Joanne needs these guidelines to be explained very clearly at times when she is feeling calm and in control. For example, the rule is that we don't scream. However, it is fine to scream at a baseball game or when someone needs help. Since Joanne needs a trusted adult to help her when she is unsure of how to behave, there is a designated "go-to person" in each setting, such as the guidance counselor at school, her soccer coach, her religious school teacher, and her parents.

With these accommodations in place, Joanne is learning to manage her initial tendency to react strongly when something unexpected happens. She is learning to calm herself, and then to generate acceptable ways to handle the situation. She is getting better at problem-solving, and the adults reinforce this by praising her when she is able to move on without incident.

your favorite place. I'll be in the kitchen. Let me know when you feel calmer and ready to tackle this again."

Transitioning From Short-Term to Long-Term Goals

Our ultimate goal is to increase children's flexibility in thinking and problem-solving. Younger children need considerable warning and preparation for changes. As kids get older, they may be able to respond to changes in a more controlled manner.

The shift from short-term to long-term strategies happens by gradually moving responsibility for problem solving from the adult to the child. This gradual shift occurs in stages based upon the child's abilities and developmental status.

First, the adult generates the intervention. ("It's raining, so we won't be able to go the playground today. Why don't we play a game together instead?")

At the next stage, the adult generates the intervention, but narrates the process of problem solving to model the behavior for the child. ("It's raining, and that means a change in plans since it's not a very good playground day. I'm really disappointed, and I guess you are, too. Let's think about some other special, fun things we could do together instead. I'm thinking that we could play a game together, or bake some cookies, or go visit Grandma. Do you have any other ideas for how to handle our change in plans?") Next, the adult might shift to just prompting the child by initiating the process. ("Look at the weather out there. What do you think that means for our plans?")

Eventually, *most* children internalize the process and need less and less adult input. Our ultimate goal is to increase children's flexibility in thinking and problem-solving. When this is not possible, we aim to have them adapt more quickly to changes and more readily accept different points of view.

Educate Others and Advocate For Your Child

Kids who are less cognitively flexible than their peers may encounter notable difficulties at school, with peers, in the community, and at home. When inflexible children or teens face transitions or unexpected events in settings away from home, their strong reactions may be hard for others to understand. While most kids we work with learn to handle these changes adequately by the time they are in middle school, some continue to need support into their middle school years and beyond. Helping others to understand the nature of your child's difficulty will pave the way for the types of accommodations that allow her to effectively deal with change. Even relatively simple accommodations, such as advance warning of what will happen, can make a big difference in the daily life of a child who struggles to be flexible.

To advocate for your child, you will need to offer your perspective on your child's behavior. ("Actually, it's not just changing classes that is likely to be difficult. Tom sometimes gets upset with smaller changes, too. Can I suggest a few techniques that seem to help?") At school, accommodations for an inflexible student can be initiated informally or may be part of a formal intervention plan. Grandparents, babysitters, sports coaches, and others who spend time with your child will benefit from your perspective, as well.

Final Thoughts

It is impossible to prepare a child for all of the possible exceptions to rules or to ready her for all unpredictable events. Of course, our goal is to help kids learn to manage these situations on their own. However, some kids with cognitive rigidity have so much difficulty that they need a higher level of support. For these children, we offer what they need to be able to manage the settings in which they must operate. Some of the interventions and supports we use to help kids who have very limited cognitive flexibility would be accurately viewed as "coddling" or "enabling" for other kids. However, while most kids can adapt to a change in the school menu, others, like Joanne, need a different approach, which will allow them to build their competence at their own developmental pace.

While all of the executive functions may be viewed as helping people effectively adapt to changing environmental demands and conditions, cognitive flexibility plays a key role in figuring out how to manage our ever-changing world. As such, it is an important focus of intervention.

13

Helping Children Get Started on Homework and Other Tasks

Initiation = The ability to independently recognize when it's time to get started on something and mobilize one's resources to do so.

The ability to begin working or get started on a task is important for school functioning, negotiating the daily routine, and maintaining social relationships. Of course, all children begin life heavily dependent on adults to let them know when it is time to begin (and end) certain activities. We don't know any two-year-olds who hop up from their play to go independently brush their teeth! However, as kids get older, we expect to see a gradual transition from external cues to trigger the "start" function to internal management of this essential executive skill. When children and adolescents lag behind peers in their initiation skills, they are very likely to be viewed as lazy or unmotivated, when, in fact, they may have specific delays in this area of development.

Strategies reviewed in this chapter help children who:

- have difficulty starting homework;
- have problems completing chores and routine activities without prompting; and
- put off major projects, even if important to them.

Below, we've listed general intervention strategies that you'll want to employ with your child who has trouble initiating tasks. Further down, we've provided advice for dealing with more specific scenarios that you're likely to experience with your child or teen. Note that depending on the issue you are addressing with your child, you will typically use only a subset of the strategies discussed in this chapter.

SUMMARY: GENERAL STRATEGIES TO HELP YOUR CHILD GET STARTED

Provide external structure in the form of general guidelines, cues, and support.

Develop schedules and routines. Once an activity becomes automatic, the need for the initiation function is significantly reduced.

Use technology. Alarms, timers, and other external aids can help cue the start function.

Start the task with your child.

Use rewards (tangible, verbal, or otherwise) to motivate desired behavior. If rewards alone do not work, you may also need to take away privileges or, when appropriate, allow the natural consequence to occur. Be sure to let your child know in advance that he may lose privileges.

Strategies to Help Your Child Get Started with Homework

1. Provide external structure in the form of general guidelines, cues, and support. For example:
   - Convey the importance of homework by laying out guidelines in accordance with your values and your child's needs. ("Jack, I think it is good for you to get some physical activity before you sit down to do your homework. So, let's plan for a half-hour of outside play time after you get home from school. Then a quick snack and you start your homework. Once you have finished your homework and your chores, you can have some 'electronic time' for video games or television.")

- Many people who have difficulty initiating tasks also have problems with planning and organizing. Their difficulty with getting started may be exacerbated by the fact that they are overwhelmed by the task and don't know where to start. They may need more guidelines and support to break down the task into component parts. (See Chapter 15: Helping Children Plan and Organize.)

2. Develop schedules and routines. For example:
   - Set up a daily homework time that is consistent from one day to the next (at least as much as other activities and demands allow). You may need to experiment a bit to determine what time works best for your child (i.e., after he's eaten a snack or had a chance to decompress after the school day).
   - Provide verbal reminders to help your child to monitor the time until the behavior becomes a routine. ("Jessie, it is three thirty now. If you want a snack, now is the time. You have fifteen minutes before homework time.")
   - Sit down together with your child each day and review his homework assignments. Plan out how long each task is likely to take and then plan out the afternoon and evening based on the homework demands and other activities.

TRY THIS!

Some children tend to rush through their homework in order to get to free time. For these children, we recommend that you designate not just a start time for homework, but a homework hour (or more, if this is an older child who tends to have more than an hour's worth of daily homework). So, homework time might be from five to six o'clock. If the child finishes his homework with time to spare, he can read a book that he picks out. Only homework and reading are allowed during the designated hour. That way, the child is less likely to rush through his work to get to video games or other preferred activities.

3. Use technology, for example:
   - A timer or watch with an alarm can be set to cue a child to begin a designated task. Watches with countdown timers can

be set so that an alarm goes off after a specific time interval, so that your child knows when play time is over and work time starts. The WatchMinder2®, a commercially available assistive device, is a digital watch that allows the child to receive reminders to complete tasks at given times. The Time Timer® and Time Tracker® Visual Timer & Clock are also excellent visual support tools that communicate the concept of elapsed time with an easy-to-understand graphic depiction of time remaining. Making the passage of time concrete, a tool like this can tell your child "how much longer?" before TV time is over and homework hour begins.

- To encourage independence, move from being the timekeeper to having the child set a timer or watch. You should probably monitor the time yourself, as well, so that you know if your child if fudging it or not. Be sure to offer lavish praise when your child starts homework without being cued!
- For older children who carry cell phones, consider using the alarm function that is often built into programs already loaded on the phone.
- Some older kids are real "techies" and might even embrace the chance to use a PDA (personal digital assistant) like a Palm Pilot or Blackberry. However, you might not want to purchase such an expensive piece of technology for a kid who loses everything!

4. Start the task with the child.
   - Some students spend an inordinate amount of time staring at their papers, just thinking, particularly when faced with a writing assignment. For such students, try talking through the assignment with them. Talk about what they will write, possible opening sentences, and then sit with them until they have started writing. Sometimes, to get them rolling, you might even try having them dictate the first sentence and you write it.

5. Use rewards and natural consequences to motivate desired behavior. For example:
   - Play "Beat the Clock": Measure how long it takes for the child to start a task once he has been given a directive. Reward the child for improving on his best time, e.g., if the child tends to sit at his desk for a long time before starting "morning work,"

chart how long it takes to get started and reward the child for reducing that time. (This would probably not be a good strategy to use with a child or adolescent who is overly anxious.)

• Reward completion of homework with the opportunity to spend time doing a preferred activity. ("Once you finish your homework you can go back outside to play if you have done a thorough job and there is still time before dinner is ready.")

• Use natural consequences to motivate behavior when those consequences are reasonable and appropriate. "Jack, homework has to be done before TV time. I know you want to watch the basketball playoffs. The game starts at eight o'clock, so get moving or you'll miss the start of the game."

Strategies to Help Your Child Complete Chores and Routine Activities

1. Provide external structure in the form of general guidelines and support. For example:
   • Provide specific deadlines and endpoints. ("You need to clear the table right after dinner" or "All your chores need to be completed by seven o'clock.")
   • Tie completion of chores to meaningful reinforcers. ("You need to clear the table and load the dishwasher before you can go play. If the table is not cleared by seven o'clock, then it will be bath time and you won't have any play time tonight.")

2. Use rewards and natural consequences to motivate desired behavior. For example:
   • Provide an additional reward for completing chores without being reminded. (If you have established a point chart or other behavior management system with concrete reinforcers, build in bonus points for self-initiation.) We provide more information about behavior modification techniques in Chapter 9: Behavior Change in a Nutshell.
   • Use natural consequences if they are reasonable and appropriate. "Janet, we need a few hours if we are going to go to the mall, and we need to be home by dinner time. So, if you want to go shopping today, you will need to be finished with your chores by three o'clock. Otherwise, we just won't have time."

TIP: Sometimes, the obvious natural consequences for a behavior are simply too undesirable. For example, if your child misses the bus repeatedly because he hits the snooze button on his alarm clock and oversleeps, you may end up driving him to school regularly. (We are assuming here that you have already tried such interventions as providing a second alarm clock placed farther away from his bed as back-up.) The natural consequence for missing the bus might be leaving him to walk to school on his own, but then he would be late. Naturally, you end up driving him. So, what would be a reasonable consequence? Think about a consequence that accounts for the extra time you devote to driving him to school. Here's how you can present this: "John, when I drive you to school, it takes me twenty minutes round trip, and that is twenty minutes that I would have used to get my own work done. So, each time I drive you to school, you owe me twenty minutes when you get home from school. You will spend those twenty minutes helping me with the housework that I usually do, like laundry or cleaning." After following through with those natural consequences a time or two, your son might want some help thinking through ways for getting an earlier start in the morning.

3. Start the task with the child.
   - Jump-start your child's activation system by starting the task with him. ("Joshua, it's time to clean up your toys. I'll pick up all the books and put them on the shelf. You start with the art supplies.")
   - Provide the needed materials and physical supervision. ("Okay, Steve. Here is your bread, peanut butter, and jelly. Once you make your sandwich, we will add a piece of fruit that you like and put everything in your lunch bag.")

Strategies to Help a Child Who Puts Off Major Projects

1. Provide external structure in the form of general guidelines and support. For example:

- Often people with initiation difficulties can talk knowledgeably about what needs to be done and the importance of the project, and then surprise us by doing nothing concrete to complete it! It is important to remember that knowing and doing are two different things. Help your child monitor concrete action towards a goal, rather than assuming that talking about what needs to be done means that the situation is under control.

- When you review daily homework with your child, be sure that due dates for tests and long-term assignments are also entered into the agenda book. Then work with your child on determining when the work needs to be started, and have him enter that as daily homework in the agenda book. Older children with major projects to complete, such as long-term projects and college applications, sometimes need help in breaking down a task and developing a timeline for completion of the steps.

- Use a single tool as the central organizing system for tracking all projects, including nonschool demands. The information might be recorded and tracked in an agenda book, on a calendar, on a white board, or in a visual mapping program on the computer. Visual mapping programs let the user brainstorm and organize ideas in a visual format. The software can convert the visual format to outline form with the press of a button. See Chapter 15: Helping Children Plan and Organize, for more information and samples of "mind maps." The important thing is that for some people with initiation difficulties, the "out of sight, out of mind" principle operates a bit too well. These folks need constant, concrete reminders of things that are due.

- As noted previously, many kids who have difficulty initiating tasks also have problems with planning and organizing. Their difficulty with getting started may be exacerbated by the fact that they are overwhelmed by the task and don't know where to start. They may need more guidelines and support to break down the task into component parts. See also Chapter 15: Helping Children Plan and Organize.

- For older children and adolescents, it can help to remove this work from the context of the parent-child relationship, and instead to engage the help of a tutor or AD/HD coach.

TRY THIS!

Just like a coach can help improve your child's gymnastics or chess skills, there are a growing number of professionals who work with children and adolescents to help build executive skills. By definition, the coaching relationship is collaborative and will be most successful for children and adolescents who are able to identify areas of weakness and who are open to experimenting with strategies to build their skills. Although many coaches who work with adults provide support via phone or email, we prefer "in-person" support for kids. The coach does not prescribe what an individual *should* do; rather, he offers flexible suggestions of what might be worth trying. Coaches come from a range of backgrounds and professions, including teaching, counseling, speech-language therapy, and occupational therapy. Some coaches are licensed in a mental health profession before seeking the training as a coach. Although there is no licensing process for AD/HD or executive coaches at this time, several organizations including the International Coach Federation (www.coachfederation.org) and the AD/HD Coaches Federation (www.adhdcoaches.org) provide credentialing and practice guidelines. Unlike tutoring, coaching does not build specific academic skills but can be very helpful in addressing problems with school performance, including initiation difficulties. Sometimes, therapists or counselors who specialize in working with people with AD/HD incorporate coaching techniques into their work.

2. Start the task with your child.
   - Working with the child on the first step of a major project may help to get the child into gear.
   - For many children who have difficulty with initiation, choosing a topic or focus from among a large range of options can be quite difficult. Just helping the child narrow the field of choices can be quite useful.
   - When possible, consider the use of teams or other small groups. For many people, the structure inherent in a group effort (e.g., breaking down the work into sub-tasks and assigning them to team members, scheduled meetings, devel-

oping a team timeline) compensates for the executive skill weaknesses. Also, working in a small group allows the person to gain momentum from the energy and focus others bring to the project. Working together with another child to earn a scouting badge, for example, works better for some children than working alone.

3. Use rewards and natural consequences to motivate desired behavior. For example:
   - Older students might benefit from setting up their own rewards for completing work. One college student we know used a concert ticket as the incentive for completing a major project on time. Here's how that worked: Jack and his friends bought tickets to see a favorite band in concert. However, the concert was the weekend before a major school project was due, and Jack knew that he often needed those last few days to finish (or even start) his work. So, Jack gave his concert ticket to a trusted friend with the instructions that the friend was only allowed to give it back if he had e-mailed the project to the professor before the concert. Otherwise, the friend was to invite someone else and use Jack's ticket. (Jack did complete the project!)
   - Trouble with initiation can have consequences outside of school, as well. Jim is a Boy Scout who has earned few badges because of his tendency to procrastinate. Jim's parents have talked with his troop leader and together they've developed a schedule with regular check-ins so that Jim can earn the badges he would like.

CASE STUDY: PUTTING IT ALL TOGETHER

Mark is a twelve-year-old boy who has many friends, but he often finds he has no one to play with. He repeatedly complains to his mom that when he does call a friend to come over, that person most often already has plans. Mark's parents have told him over and over again that he needs to plan in advance, and he always says he will do that. However, his parents are frustrated because he does not follow through.

(continued on next page)

(continued from previous page)

Fortunately, his parents recognize that he is motivated to do well and do not blame him for his initiation weaknesses. Still, it can be quite frustrating to try to help him as he knows what he should do, talks about what he needs to do, but has trouble with the "doing." Mark missed out on playing with friends because he didn't initiate invitations and he did not plan ahead to see when his friends would be available. Despite his parents' repeated suggestions that he do so, Mark did not follow through with his stated intent to call friends.

Mark's parents started taking a more active role in helping him to just do it. Whenever he complained to his mom that he was bored and wanted someone to do things with, she worked with him to set it up. She helped him to identify who he wanted to invite over, and then she reminded him of the right-now approach. "Do it right now, so that it gets done." She sat down with him while he called his friend. She encouraged him to be ready with a number of different options, so that while the friend was on the phone they could make alternate plans if the initial proposal did not work.

Mark's parents also reviewed the calendar with him every Monday afternoon. They found that a free "on-line" calendar worked best; he also was able to keep a list of friends' addresses and phone numbers. Looking ahead for the week, they identified the afternoon and weekend times that Mark would be available to play. Their Monday routine included calling friends to arrange for at least one weekday and one weekend time with a friend. Planning in advance meant that his friends were more often available, and so the natural rewards reinforced the behavior of initiating the calls. He also benefited from the email reminders that he could set using the internet calendar program.

After a while, the Monday routine became part of the weekly ritual, and Mark initiated it with only occasional reminders.

Still, on a variety of tasks at home and at school, Mark's parents and teachers continue to provide a relatively high level of external prompting and support. They recognize that his internal "start" switch is hard to trigger and that his lack of initiation and resulting procrastination are due to executive weaknesses rather than insufficient motivation.

Transitioning From Short-Term to Long-Term Goals

When children or teens have difficulty with initiation, we first build routines and reinforce the children for sticking with them. We create a structure for important activities, such as when homework needs to be done, and we maintain active involvement in seeing that the child adheres to the structure. Often, as routines kick in, the struggle over initiating a particular task diminishes. Over time, you should do less direct prompting ("Jack, start your homework.") and instead prompt the child to think about the rule ("Jack, it's four o'clock. What is the rule about homework time?") The next step is to prompt the child to use strategies to activate himself. ("Jack, how about you set your watch alarm for 3:55 p.m. That will be your cue to come inside and start doing your homework at four o'clock.")

In order to move toward the long-term goal of building independence, people who struggle with initiation need to learn to regularly use tools, such as watches, schedules, and calendars. Gadgets, tools, and systems only work if the person has good habits using them, so we reinforce the child for repeatedly using them.

We also want our kids to gradually broaden their focus so that they move from thinking about a particular task (e.g., doing today's homework) to developing effective ways of managing demands in general (e.g., daily consideration of the schedule and what needs to get done). ("Jack, did you make a list on your white board of the things that need to get done today?") We move from suggesting a strategy, to encouraging the child to come up with one on their own. ("Jack, do you have a plan for getting started with your science project?")

We need to continue to heighten the child or teen's awareness of how long things take and the importance of thinking in terms of timeframes. ("Jack, we are leaving on Saturday for vacation. What is your schedule like this week? When do you plan to start your packing?") Even when a kid has developed pretty good routines that help him get started, be prepared to provide help from time to time, particularly during times of increased stress. ("Jack, I know that moving to a new house so close to final exams isn't going to be easy; let's figure out how I can help without nagging.")

Perhaps most importantly, we encourage people with initiation difficulties to shift from vague plans, ("Oh, I don't know, I guess I'll do it sometime Thursday or Friday afternoon.") to specific deadlines ("I'll be home from football practice at two o'clock, so I'll shower and start my packing by three o'clock."). As one professional project planner recently stated so succinctly, "Nothing ever gets done without a deadline."

As your child matures, and as he learns from experience about his own tendency to wait too long, to start too late, and to come up short, we gently call upon his experience to help him understand his own profile and to inspire new approaches. ("Jack, my last-minute son, I just don't see how you will be done packing on time if you don't get started really soon. Remember the last time we went on a trip? You were so surprised by how long it took to get ready and you were racing around at the last minute. You got really frustrated because you forgot your favorite game and your cell phone charger. That was so unpleasant. What do you think would be a better way to handle this?")

Overall, what we are doing is a form of scaffolding—teaching skills that build on each other and that work together to allow the person to reach a higher level of performance. Your child may start to balk at your involvement, and that is an opportunity for you to re-consider whether you are doing too much. Give him some room to show you what he can do on his own. If you need reminders of the guidelines for how to adjust expectations, take a look at Chapter 10 again.

With maturation, experience, and teaching, we have seen many children and teens rise to the challenge of starting tasks in a more timely manner. However, we have also seen children and adolescents who continue to need external prompts and reminders for years before they develop sufficient independent activation skills. You may need to continue to "flip the switch" by using verbal prompts and reminding him to take advantage of his calendar, schedule, or technology.

Difficulty with initiation can be a stubborn problem. Some people with significant executive weakness continue to need a high level of support to help them start important tasks through high school and even beyond. Achieving independence may sometimes require finding someone other than yourself, the parent, to be an accountability partner and to help your child set and stick to his own deadlines. Procrastination is often the issue that leads adults with AD/HD to seek counseling or coaching!

Educate Others and Advocate for Your Child

Kids with initiation or activation weaknesses may be viewed as "passive," "lazy," "unmotivated," or "dependent." If these are the words you've heard to describe your child, you may need to share what you have learned about him with his school or the other adults involved with your family. Providing a copy of the evaluation report that describes your child's profile may be helpful.

Sometimes, initiation difficulties are more apparent at home than at school, since the classroom setting is more structured with fewer options for when things get done. Share your observations with your child's teacher and discuss possible interventions that will help with homework, such as breaking large tasks into smaller chunks and having interim deadlines for portions of larger projects. This may include first turning in an outline, then making a timeline for each part of a paper or project.

Be cautious about the use of natural consequences. Sometimes, natural consequences serve as powerful motivation, leading to the development of important new learning. However, when the child or teen simply does not have the skills to perform the desired behavior, then natural consequences (such as failing a class) may be unreasonable. Sometimes, without some careful observation of his hits and misses, we don't know if a youngster has acquired a specific ability. For example, one teenaged client looked forward excitedly to his first band trip with the middle school. While he talked about what he needed to take and eagerly showed his mom the packing list that had been given to all the kids, he seemed to get nothing accomplished toward being ready to leave. So, it seems unlikely that this young boy was being "lazy" or "unmotivated." Stepping in to help him get started was the obvious and most effective solution for this situation. (For the next band trip, however, it would be more helpful to develop a "packing plan" in advance, with target dates for specific tasks that need to get done in order to be ready to go.)

While we do not want children to suffer unreasonably harsh consequences for behaviors they do not yet have the ability to change, as parents, we must be mindful of our tendency to work too hard to protect our children from the world. We must be open to examining our own actions to make sure we are doing the best job we can to promote independence.

When you can collaborate with other adults in your child's life (your spouse, life partner, school staff, etc.), you will have the best chance of effectively thinking through what will help your child move forward and become more independent. If your child's difficulties with initiation are interfering significantly with learning or performance in the school setting, he may need school-based instruction and/or accommodations through an informal plan or more formally through Special Education services or a 504 Plan.

Final Thoughts

We can all think of times when we just couldn't start on something that needed to be done. Often it is the looming deadline that finally launches us into action. This is also true for kids with executive weaknesses, but the frequency and intensity of the problem is on a different scale. Since people with executive weaknesses have difficulty keeping the long-term picture in mind, more immediate consequences help them get started.

Parents often have questions about whether their child is choosing to avoid a task or is having real difficulty getting started. Wouldn't anybody rather watch TV than take out the trash? Fortunately, many of the ways to help kids get started work equally well whether executive weakness or avoidance is the underlying issue. However, it is true that some kids, in fact a significant percentage of kids with AD/HD, show a pattern of oppositional behavior. If your child seems to have a significant problem with oppositional behavior, you may need to learn specific interventions for noncompliance that are outside the scope of this book. (Dr. Russell Barkley's books on defiant children are quite useful.) However, you should first try the types of interventions offered here, since many of the ways to help kids get started work equally well whether executive weakness or avoidance is the underlying issue.

14

Helping Children Handle Working Memory Issues

Working memory = The ability to temporarily hold information in one's head in order to use it to complete a task.

Working memory is best understood as an internal scratch pad. It provides us with a place to store information that we will need to use for the next step of a task, but that we do not need to store beyond that time. For those with weak working memories, it is as if their scratch pads are much smaller than expected, so that they cannot hold as much information in mind as others do. Further, the lettering on the scratch pad seems to be written in disappearing ink, so the words or images fade more quickly than for others. It's easy to see how not having an adequate internal scratch pad can make managing many of life's tasks difficult.

This is particularly troublesome because so much everyday information is communicated orally. We give directions or other information out loud, and we just expect that the listener will hold on to what we say. However, words are a fading stimulus that may leave the listener's awareness as soon as the sound waves dissipate. Information presented orally leaves no trail; that is, there is nothing concrete to re-inspect when the listener needs to review the information.

Another problem for those with weak working memories is that it is hard to think creatively at the same time that they are trying to remember the directions for the task. The child may falter on some tasks because of the complexity involved in holding on to the information from the directions, generating creative ideas in response, and then adding the specifics of how to express those thoughts. The scratch pad is simply overloaded!

Strategies reviewed in this chapter help children who:

- have trouble following directions;
- have trouble with written expression and other complex, multi-step tasks;
- interrupt others so they won't forget what they want to say;
- need to re-read or re-learn information – it just doesn't stick; and
- have trouble taking notes in class.

Below, we've listed general intervention strategies that you'll want to employ with your child or student who has trouble remembering things. Further down, we've provided advice for dealing with more specific scenarios that you're likely to experience with your child or teen. Note that depending on the issue you are addressing with your child, you will typically use only a subset of the strategies discussed in this chapter.

SUMMARY: GENERAL STRATEGIES TO HELP YOUR CHILD WITH WORKING MEMORY ISSUES

Modify the presentation of information so that it is more easily remembered

Use multisensory strategies such as pairing verbal instructions with visual cues. Multisensory teaching is the process of connecting multiple sensory inputs to the material to be learned. This is done using strategies that connect new learning with input from the eyes, ears, voice, and/or hands.

Teach strategies and techniques to aid recall, such as mnemonics.

Provide templates for procedures or routines that are repeated.

Teach the use of concrete storage systems that create an external scratch pad and so take the burden off the weak internal storage system.

Accommodate working memory weaknesses by providing reasonable supports.

Strategies to Help a Child Who Has Trouble Following Directions

1. Modify the presentation of information so that it is more easily remembered. For example:

   - Organize and simplify the directions.

     ➤ Organize the information in a manner that creates bullet points to aid in recall. ("Remember, you have *three* important points to write about: What was the problem, how did the people solve it, and what was the outcome. Remember, I want to see three points." Or "Johnny, this morning we have some clean-up chores to do around the house before we can go swimming. You have *three* things you need to get done. Here they are: First, put all the dirty clothes into your hamper. Second, bring the hamper down to the laundry room. Third, put your superhero guys away. Got it? There are three things on your list. Do you remember what they are? You tell me so I am sure you've got them all.")

     ➤ Simplify the directions so that the most important information stands out. "Jackie, I want you to get your coat, get your library books from the dining room table, and come back here to the kitchen. Got that? Coat. Library books. Kitchen. Go."

TIP: To organize and simplify directions, you need to distill the most important information to convey to your child. This means that you must eliminate extraneous information, such as what it means for your child's long-term development if she does not clean her room, how what she does reflects on her character, or how you had to walk four miles through the snow to get to school when you were a child. Okay, we know that's an exaggeration of the process, but you get the point. Simplifying the message is a good thing because otherwise your child will get lost in the words and in the complex emotions and worries that you convey. Focus on the here-and-now, and you automatically narrow in on the most important information.

2. Use multisensory strategies to aid recall. Multisensory teaching is the process of connecting multiple sensory inputs to the material to be learned. This is done using strategies that connect new learning with input from the eyes, ears, voice, and/or hands. For example:

- "Let's sing the directions."
- "Tap the table for each step you need to do."
- "Let's make a picture list of all the things we need to get done before Grandma and Grandpa get here."

TRY THIS!

Set your simplified directions to song, rhythm, or dance steps. If you have a playful style to begin with, capture that occasional, spontaneous silliness to punctuate your serious parental efforts. A few verses of "Shoes, coat, cha-cha-cha" with the accompanying dance steps may help you all get out the door with smiles on your faces!

3. Teach strategies and techniques to compensate for working memory weaknesses. For example:

- Teach the child to visualize. "So you have to pack for your ski trip. Imagine yourself walking through a whole day of vacation and think about what you will need from the time you wake up until you go to bed and then get each item as you think about it." You might even suggest that the child make a list while she's sitting there visualizing, and *then* have her collect each item and check it off the list. If your child is younger or needs more support, offer to be the list-maker while she dictates the list. You can check off each item as she packs it.
- Teach the child to repeat directions several times in her head in order to lock in the information. ("Turn to page fifteen and get out my notebook and pencil. Page fifteen, notebook, pencil. Page fifteen, notebook, pencil.")
- Teach the student to read the directions softly to herself both before and after completing the assignments. ("After you complete your test, reread all of the directions and make sure you have done all that is expected.")

- Teach your child to use mnemonic devices in the form of short rhymes or special words to recall lists. ("You can remember the line notes in the treble clef by repeating 'Every **g**ood **b**oy **d**eserves **f**udge.'" Or, "Remember the list of stuff I'd like you to pick up at the store by thinking of the word "beam": **b**read, **e**ggs, **a**pples, **m**ilk.")

4. **Provide templates for procedures or routines that are repeated.** A template lays out the standard steps to complete a repetitive task and can be useful for a variety of home and school demands. Templates are particularly helpful for those who have trouble with planning/organizing in addition to working memory weakness. The templates can be faded out when the procedure becomes automatic. However, this should be monitored carefully so that the template can be brought back if it appears that it was faded too soon. For example:
   - Use chore cards to keep your child on task, as suggested by Dr. Russell Barkley. These index cards list the steps to complete a particular job. You and your child can create a chore card together when you first introduce a new job. A simple numbered list of all the parts of a task works well. For example, to clean up the child's room:
     1. Throw away trash
     2. Put dirty clothes in hamper
     3. Put clean clothes away
     4. Books on bookshelf
     5. Toys in correct put-away place
     6. Make bed

     Then, at chore time, you hand the child the card for the chore to complete. "Byron, here is your chore card for this morning. Just follow the steps on the card. Bring the card back to me when you finish the chore."
   - Provide a template for specific academic skills. For example, create a template that lays out the steps for long division. This relieves the student of needing to remember the steps at the same time that she is trying to understand the process of division.
   - For daily routines, create checklists. This can be helpful for kids who tend to leave out steps when packing their backpacks, doing their basic morning hygiene routines, settling into the classroom, or packing up materials that will be needed at home.

5. Teach the use of concrete external storage systems to take the burden off of the internal working memory. For example:

- For young children, make a to-do list or schedule using pictures. This can also help kids who have trouble keeping track of steps in their morning and evening routines. These can even be laminated so the child can use a dry erase marker to check off each step as it is completed. This visual component illustrates competence to the child and ultimately builds confidence and motivates future success.

- Teach your child to write down oral information. The written information becomes a concrete cue that can be re-inspected whenever necessary after oral recall fades. For example:
  - ➤ "Marina, I need you to run into the grocery store and get a few things while I pick up the dry cleaning next door. Do you have some paper? Great! Here are the four things we need. Write them down."
  - ➤ "Richard, I agree that you need a new notebook. You also mentioned yesterday that you need some socks. Write the things you need on the white board in your room so you will remember to pick them up when we next go shopping."

- Teach your child or teen to jot down a few notes as the teacher is giving oral directions. Writing down a few key words can ensure that she is doing the requested problems and not wasting her time on the wrong page.

- Use technology to compensate for weak working memory. For example, "When you think of something you need to do, record a message on your cell phone, send yourself a reminder email, or call your voicemail and leave a message."

- Ask your child's teachers if they are okay with having their lectures recorded. For a child who has difficulty focusing on what is being said while writing notes, having a recording that can be stopped and started can be a big help.

6. Accommodate working memory weaknesses by providing reasonable supports. For example:

- Expect to repeat the directions, as necessary, and do so in a patient, sensitive manner.

- For adolescents, ask how you can provide reminders or cues without bugging them. Be flexible and willing to try any reasonable way of helping.

- Prompt for good listening skills. ("I am going to give you the directions. Please look at me so I know that you are focusing.")
- Request accommodations in the classroom that focus on creating back-up for your child's weak memory. These could include such interventions as having the teacher provide a written copy of directions and assignments, and having the teacher review and initial the student's agenda book to indicate that the assignment has been written down fully and correctly and that nothing has been omitted.
- Teach your child the importance of having the phone numbers of at least two students in the class so she has someone to call if she needs to check on an assignment. Teach your child to select kids who are good students, not necessarily a best buddy if the buddy also forgets what the buddy was supposed to do!
- Offer understanding and support when the child experiences frustration or failure, for example:
  - ➤ "It is hard to keep track of doing so many things at once. Would it help if I make a list so you can check off each step?"
  - ➤ "Sometimes it is hard to manage complicated directions. Let's read these aloud and then take it one step at a time."
  - ➤ "I am sorry that you spent so long and worked so hard on your project, but your teacher pointed out that you didn't complete the essay. Let's see if she will give you a second chance to finish it."

TIP: Sometimes, parents avoid talking with their children about the difficult feelings and frustrations the children experience, living with weak executive skills. If you cannot talk about these emotions, then your child may feel that her feelings are too scary even for you to acknowledge. Model for your child that even difficult feelings can be looked at and discussed objectively. Validate your child's feelings with a simple observation. "You look really sad." Or, "I'm guessing that you are really frustrated by that grade." This gives her an opportunity to say more, if she chooses, and helps her feel less alone with her feelings. It is not your job, nor is it possible, for you to take away her feelings. Your job is to listen, to try to understand, and to help her think about how to handle the situation.

Strategies to Help a Child with Written Expression and Other Complex, Multi-Step Tasks

1. Teach the use of concrete external storage systems to take the burden off of the internal working memory. For example:
   - Separate the process of brainstorming ideas from the mechanics of completing the project. Teach the child to take notes, either manually or using brainstorming software, while formulating ideas. For younger children, you may want to take notes while you talk together about their ideas. Some students benefit from voice-to-text software that allows them to talk into a microphone connected to their computers, while the computer creates a text file of these mental notes. (There are many voice-to-text software programs available commercially. All require some time to train the computer to understand the idiosyncrasies of an individual's voice, but the programs have improved substantially over the years.)
   - Those with working memory difficulties benefit from some of the same software that helps folks with planning and organization difficulties. Such programs, designed for brainstorming and organizing ideas into a visual schema, are great for capturing thoughts that evaporate too quickly from the minds of those with weak working memories. Such programs as Kidspiration®, Inspiration®, and Mindjet MindManager® are great tools for laying out written assignments. (See Figure 14.1.) More examples of how this software can be helpful appear in Chapter 15: Helping Children Plan and Organize.
   - Many schools now teach students to create visual organizers as the first step of the writing process. This is a way of formulating ideas and then working with those ideas to create a written response. The concrete visual format helps to reduce the amount of information that must be kept in mind while creating the response. Learn what types of visual organizers are being used in your child's classroom so that you can support this learning and use the same techniques at home.

2. Provide templates for procedures or routines that are repeated. For example:
   - Templates for writing tasks can be a valuable tool for some students. They free the student from needing to think about

Figure 14.1

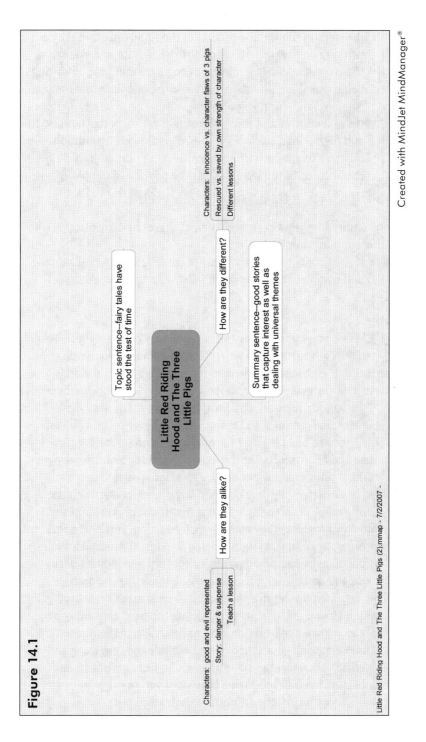

Created with MindJet MindManager®

the steps in the writing process at the same time that they are working on the content of the written assignment. For example, a student can be taught to recognize what type of writing is being called for, and then to choose the template that fits (e.g., compare-and-contrast paper, persuasive essay, etc.). An experienced educational professional that we know teaches middle and high school students to use Power Point©, Inspiration®, or other software for writing, because it cues the user to choose the purpose of the writing and then provides a template that walks through the steps to achieve the desired product.

3. Accommodate working memory weaknesses by providing reasonable supports. For example:
   - If your child's oral responses are consistently more elaborate and complete than her minimalist written work would

TIP: It makes good sense to teach children keyboarding skills in the early elementary years. Using a computer for writing saves the child from having to re-copy work when she adds to it or corrects it. The computer also provides opportunities for various software options that make written work less burdensome. Learning to keyboard can be quite tedious so you may need to build in some meaningful reinforcers for adequate time and effort practicing this skill. Some kids do best working with a tutor or occupational therapist for several sessions to make sure that they develop good finger positioning. There are also a range of software programs that teach keyboarding and monitor progress. They come in many different versions, some incorporating elements with inherent interest to the child, such as popular videogame characters or sports game formats. Many kids will do best with reinforcers for completing the practice necessary to master this skill. Many schools teach keyboarding, although you might want to accelerate the pace of learning by teaching your child at home or making it a summer project. Consider asking your school what software they are using and perhaps obtaining the same program. In fact, some software publishers have arrangements that allow you to order software through the school at a discounted price.

suggest, consider requesting accommodations that help her get those thoughts onto paper. Request that the school allow your child to dictate responses to you for homework assignments. You can take notes or type the information into the computer, and then your child can work from those notes. This does not mean that you write the paper for the child—your job is simply to serve as a scribe or note-taker.

Strategies to Help a Child Who Interrupts Others So She Won't Forget What She Wants to Say

1. Provide external structure to facilitate working memory. For example:
   - "Tell me your question now and when I am done talking, I will answer it."

2. Teach the use of concrete storage systems that create an external scratch pad and so take the burden off the weak internal storage system. For example:
   - "Here's a notepad. Jot down a few words to remind you of what you want to say, and it will be your turn to talk once I am done."

Strategies to Help a Child Who Needs to Re-Read or Re-Learn Information – It Just Doesn't Stick

1. Modify the presentation of information so that it is more easily remembered. For example:
   - Introduce new material by previewing what will be presented. This creates a structure that will help the student to organize and retain new information. ("We are going to be talking about three important events in the Civil War.") Use the structure to keep the student oriented as you continue. ("So, that was the first of the three important events that we are talking about today. Now, let's talk about the second one.")
   - The same approach helps for nonacademic material. ("Listen up, Sally. I need to tell you about the choices for what we can do tomorrow when your cousins are here. I thought of three

things you all might enjoy. Here's what I came up with....So that was my second idea. Here is the third.")

2. Use multisensory strategies. Multisensory teaching is the process of connecting multiple sensory inputs to the material to be learned. This is done using strategies that connect new learning with input from the eyes, ears, voice, and/or hands. For example:
   - Some kids who have trouble remembering what they read benefit from hearing the material out loud. For these students, listening to recorded books, being read to, or even just reading the material out loud can improve learning.
   - "Let's sing the multiplication tables to the tune of 'Old Mac-Donald Had a Farm.'"
   - Active, hands-on learning experiences can be a real boost for students who do not learn as well from reading. When possible, offer options to students that allow for diverse learning styles. For example, rather than requiring everyone to write a report about dinosaurs, perhaps children could be given options such as creating a model of two dinosaurs to illustrate how they are alike and how they are different, creating a poster, or even writing and performing a play.

3. Teach strategies and techniques to aid recall. For example:
   - Teach the use of mnemonics, specific aids for memory. A common mnemonic is to attach a list to be remembered to a word that is easily remembered; each letter of the word is associated with a list item. For example, one mnemonic that is commonly used for remembering all of the Great Lakes is HOMES: **H**uron, **O**ntario, **M**ichigan, **E**rie, and **S**uperior. Encourage students to develop their own shortcuts to memorize facts, lists, and other rote information. For example, "The plan for understanding what you read is SQRRR: **S**urvey, **Q**uestion, **R**ead, **R**ecite, **R**eview."
   - Encourage the child to be an active learner by teaching ways to work with the material as she reads it. ("When you read, write a one sentence summary after reading each paragraph and put it on a sticky note. At the end, you will have a summary.")
   - Teach the child to use a highlighter to underline key words and points. The student may need a demonstration to determine what to highlight.

- Teach the student to preview the material before jumping in to reading. The goal is to create a sort of general framework upon which she can hang the specifics of what she reads. ("Let's go through first and read all of the subheadings, look at any pictures, and read text boxes.")
- Teach the student to orient herself before reading a chapter by first reading the questions at the end of the chapter.

Strategies to Help a Child Who Has Trouble Taking Notes in Class

1. Accommodate working memory weaknesses by providing reasonable supports. For students with weak working memories, it can be very difficult to listen for learning and to write at the same time. For these students, taking notes may impede learning, and the notes that they do take are likely to be incomplete.
   - Set up a system for getting the day's notes from a peer buddy or from the teacher. This should be set up as a daily routine, rather than expecting the student to make the choice each day and then to arrange to get the notes.
   - Allow the student to use a voice recorder to record the day's lecture, and then she can review it later and take notes at home. Note that this requires a lot of extra time at home to review the day's learning. Not all students are willing or able to put in that much extra time.
   - Make the note-taking process easier and more productive by providing an outline at the beginning of the class with space for the student to fill in specific information. This serves as a preview of the new material and also highlights the important information that the teacher is expecting the student to take away from the lesson. Looking at that outline later also allows the student and the adults to determine whether or not the student has gotten all the most important information written down.
   - Minimize copying from the board. This seems like such a straightforward task, but can be very difficult for some students. Copying from the board requires students to keep information in their heads as they transfer it from the board to the paper. The children have to keep track of what they last wrote, keep that in mind as they look back up at the board, find where they left off, look at the next few letters or words,

carry the information back to the paper, and keep it in their heads long enough to finish writing it down.

➤ Request that your child be assigned a "note buddy," a child in the class who takes complete notes and makes them available for your child to photocopy.

➤ Ask the teacher to provide a copy of her own notes for the day's lesson.

➤ Ask the teacher if a "study guide" outlining the main points will be a part of the end-of-unit study packet. Study guides allow the student to review what the teacher feels is the most important information from the unit.

CASE STUDY: PUTTING IT ALL TOGETHER

Sarah is a bright and delightful young teen who has significant trouble keeping track of directions. Her parents and teachers are quite frustrated because she doesn't seem able to remember more than one thing at a time. At home, her parents may assign a few chores and find, hours later, that she has done only one or two of them, saying she forgot about the others. Although she learned to read easily and understands what she reads at a high level, she sometimes reads a chapter or two in a book and can barely recall what she just read. She asks people to repeat things so often that it becomes tiresome. At school, Sarah often starts assignments but then strays from the directions. Before she knows it, her written work is far off the mark from what the teacher requested. At other times, she expresses creative and interesting comments during classroom discussions, but when it comes time to write down her ideas, the product is overly simplistic. What can be done to help Sarah?

Her behavior is confusing to her parents and teachers, as well as herself. A psycho-educational evaluation reveals that a weak working memory is the source of so many of Sarah's difficulties. Now that they understand the nature of the problem, the seemingly diverse set of challenges she presents starts to make more sense.

Sarah's parents are learning to give directions in a much more intentional manner, making the specific directions much clearer and double checking to be certain that Sarah is processing the information. When several steps are involved, they prompt her to write them down. They know that Sarah is making progress when her mom asks her to complete a few chores while she goes to do some errands. With a smile, Sarah responds, "Mom, if you really want me to do them, write them down. You know that's the only way I'll get it all done." Sarah keeps a small notebook in her purse, so that she always has scratch paper for notes and a place to keep random bits of information that she might otherwise forget, such as hastily offered information like phone numbers or the time and location for the movie outing with her friends. Although she is not allowed to have her cell phone at school, Sarah is experimenting with the voice memo function and finds it useful when she has a brief shopping list or wants to take down directions or a phone number.

Sarah's mom is experimenting, too. On a few occasions, in her more relaxed and playful moments, she created rap verses that incorporated the information Sarah needed to remember. Sarah and her mom had fun, and the rap format was quite a success. Of course, she can't always make mundane tasks that entertaining!

When it comes to school work, Sarah is gradually learning to highlight the directions on worksheets and other assignments, and to re-check her highlighting to stay on the right track. She and her teachers have found ways for her to get copies of the class notes when there is new or important material presented.

Sarah also finds that the computer really makes her life easier. She uses it for taking notes as she reads, first creating a sort of outline from the chapter headings and sub-headings. In addition to creating notes as she reads, typing the information into her computer seems to lock the information more firmly in her mind. Sarah also uses the computer for brainstorming her ideas as she starts papers or projects. The habit of brainstorming first, rather than just jumping in to the writing, has been slow to develop. Sarah now works with a tutor who incorporates these recommendations into their sessions. Although she initially balked at what she saw as extra work, as she began to get better grades on her papers and to get used to the routine, her attitude has slowly changed.

Sarah still needs reminders, at times, to use the strategies and tools that she has learned. Her parents sometimes get frustrated with her forgetfulness but they are all relieved at her progress and much more hopeful about her ability to deal with the demands of her life.

Transitioning From Short-Term to Long-Term Goals

As with other areas of executive functioning, the key to building independence is to gradually transfer responsibility for self-management to the child. Kids with weak working memories need to understand just what that means, at an age-appropriate level, so that they can understand how it affects them and what to do about it.

At first, you initiate the strategies, all the while teaching the child about her own cognitive processing profile. ("Elly, I'm going to write down the things that you need to do because you tend to forget stuff when there is a lot on your list." "Amanda, you need to do a web to plan what you will include in your paragraph. That way you can remember all your good ideas when it is time to write.")

The next step is to prompt the child to use the strategies that she has learned. ("Janelle, that is a lot of information to remember. How are you going to keep track of all that information?")

Collaborate with your child to think through the rough spots. ("Kwai, do you think it would help you to learn your lines if we make an audio recording of the scenes you will be in? Then you could listen to your lines while you read them. If you'd like, we can play the CD in the car when we are driving to and from soccer practice. Can you think of anything else that might help?")

As kids start using strategies on their own, your job shifts to one of monitoring and troubleshooting as problems arise. Sometimes, you will be the voice of reality as your child tries to do things the "easy way" rather than taking the extra steps involved in actively, systematically initiating strategies to compensate for weak working memory.

This is not a short-term project! Expect this to be a process that occurs over years as your child grows and matures.

Educate Others and Advocate for Your Child

It is easy to misinterpret signs of working memory deficits as attempts to willfully ignore directions. Teach family, sports coaches, school staff, and others working with your child about working memory and how weakness in this foundation skill affects learning and performance. Give them information to read. If your child has been tested, consider sharing your child's evaluation report or giving specific examples of her working memory capacity (e.g., "She could only repeat four digits; most kids her age can easily manage six or seven."). Many schools are familiar with the challenges posed by deficits in working memory. If not, offer to arrange an in-service presentation for a staff day or through your school's parent organization.

You may need to request special accommodations for your child at school and in other settings, as well. Ask others to write down important information. ("Ms. Baker, could you please write down those directions for Jack's clarinet practice? I'm not sure that he will remember which scales to practice and what pieces he should work on. Also, you said something about how many times to run through each song. Please write that down, too.") If your child has a formal intervention plan at school, request that they incorporate the types of strategies reviewed in this chapter.

Final Thoughts

Providing the necessary supports for a child with weak working memory requires conscious effort on the part of the adults. We are used to giving directives orally, and we presume that our message is perceived and carried forward. As therapists, we have had to learn to move out of talking mode and provide written back-up regarding agreed on goals and strategies for individuals who come to us with weak working memories. As one seven-year-old said recently, "We talk about stuff in here and it all makes sense, but then I go home and I can't remember what I agreed to do. Maybe we should write it on a sticky note and I could put it up on my wall." That is a young girl who is learning to compensate for her own weaknesses!

15

Helping Children Plan and Organize

Planning and Organization = The ability to manage current and future-oriented task demands in a systematic, efficient manner.

People with weaknesses in planning and organization have trouble independently imposing structure and order on tasks and on ideas. So, they may have difficulty organizing information in their heads, as well as organizing their stuff or planning out a long-term project. When faced with a task, they have difficulty systematically thinking through the steps required, and they tend to underestimate the complexity and the time needed.

These folks also tend to have trouble seeing the natural organizational framework within a body of information. Not surprisingly, then, they have difficulty prioritizing information and focusing on the most important points. For example, they may read a chapter of a book but then have difficulty outlining what they have read. Their summaries tend to be a recounting of details, rather than an orderly synopsis of the main themes bolstered by supporting details.

Strategies reviewed in this chapter help children who:

- neglect to turn in completed assignments;
- arrive at an event completely unprepared;
- underestimate the effort involved in a project;

- are overwhelmed at juggling multiple projects and classes;
- have trouble identifying the most important information; and
- have trouble organizing space.

Below, we've listed general intervention strategies that you'll want to employ with your child or student who finds planning and organizing difficult. Further down, we've provided advice for dealing with more specific scenarios that you're likely to experience with your child or teen. Note that depending on the issue you are addressing with your child, you will typically use only a subset of the strategies discussed in this chapter.

SUMMARY: GENERAL STRATEGIES TO HELP YOUR CHILD ORGANIZE AND PLAN

Break down tasks into component parts and provide a checklist for each component.

Offer organizational frameworks in advance that help students organize new material in their heads

Teach the use of tricks and technology that help to compensate for organizational weaknesses.

Develop templates for repetitive procedures.

Walk through the planning process with the child, and help him plan an approach to the task at hand.

Provide accommodations at home and at school.

Strategies to Help a Child Who Does Homework but Doesn't Turn It In

1. Walk through the process with the child. For example:
   - There are many different ways that someone can get off-track in the process of getting homework from home to the teacher. Talk through the process with the student. Is the homework getting lost at home? Is the homework getting lost in the bottom of the backpack or the bottom of the locker? Is it in the proper notebook, but forgotten in the pro-

cess of settling into the classroom? Once you have identified the sticking point, consider what needs to be added to the routine to get past it.

- For those who lose track of homework at home, consider instituting the following routine (from *Enabling Disorganized Students to Succeed*, by Suzanne Stevens): "Homework is not done until your homework is in its proper folder or notebook, the folders and notebooks are packed into your backpack, and your backpack is on its launching pad." Try different ways of organizing homework to find the one that best suits your child. Some students do best with a separate homework folder so that everything that needs to be turned in is organized into one place. Others do better when they organize the homework by subject. If the teachers have set up a system that does not work for your child, talk with them about allowing alternatives. This can also be done as part of a formal individualized plan, like a 504 plan.

2. Develop templates of repetitive procedures. For example:
   - Teachers can create a checklist of things to be done upon entering or leaving the classroom.
   - Parents can create written checklists or photo charts for completing chores, preparing to catch the bus in the morning, gathering necessary stuff for sports practice, etc.

3. Provide accommodations. For example:
   - Involve your child's teacher(s) in building in reminders until the desired pattern of behavior (e.g., turning in homework as soon as the student walks into the classroom) becomes a habit. Teachers understandably balk at the idea of taking on responsibility for your child's job of turning in his work. However, repeated performance of a behavior is what makes it a habit; once the behavior is automatic, then the burden is lifted from the executive system. If you help the teacher to see this as a step in the process of building independent skills, with the prospect of fading out the teacher's prompting, it may encourage the teacher to get on board.

4. Teach the use of tricks and technology that help compensate for organizational weaknesses. For example:

- If the agenda book is the primary organizing tool for tracking assignments, it could also serve as a way to remind the student to turn in assignments. For example, after completing an assignment, the student could be taught to enter a note into the next day's assignments block for that subject. Then, at the end of class, when the student enters that night's homework assignment, he will see the reminder to turn in what is due that day.
- Several versions of watches are available that can be set to vibrate and show a reminder phrase at the programmed time. "Turn in homework" can be a programmed reminder set to go off at the beginning or end of the class period. Cell phones often have an alarm function, as well, that can be set for reminder alarms. If this trick works for your child, talk to your child's teachers about allowing cell phones in the classroom for this explicit function only.
- When the student prints out an assignment at home, prompt the child to also email it to the teacher and the child's own web-based email account. Then, if the hard copy is misplaced, the child can print it out during class (with the teacher's permission) or during free time.

TRY THIS!

Few problems are as frustrating for parents and kids as not receiving credit for homework that was actually completed on time but never turned in! One tried and true behavioral strategy to remedy this is to link an already established habit to one that your child needs help acquiring. To illustrate, Ivan is a seventh grader who forgets almost everything—except his peanut butter and jelly sandwich!—when he leaves home in the morning to catch the school bus. With daily reminders from his parents, he puts his homework folder on top of his lunch in the refrigerator before going to bed each school night. Then, putting the folder in his backpack, along with his PB&J, is a "no-brainer." Ivan not only gets credit for his completed work but also learns how to creatively generate ways to manage his weaknesses.

Strategies to Help a Child Who Arrives at Sports Practice (or Other Event or Activity) Unprepared

1. Walk through the planning process with your child. For example:
    *   Think aloud with your child, going through the steps required to get all the necessary stuff to soccer practice. When you come home from soccer practice, where does the bag go? What needs to be taken out of the bag? Where do the dirty clothes go? How and when will the clean clothes get back into the soccer bag? If there is mud on the cleats, where will they go and how will they get back into the soccer bag? How will the soccer bag get to the car? Develop a consistent routine and provide support until the process becomes automatic and independent.

2. Develop templates of repetitive procedures.
    *   Make a checklist together of everything that needs to be in the soccer bag when your child arrives at practice. Laminate the list and keep it in the soccer bag for a last minute check before the bag goes into the car.

Strategies to Help a Child Who Underestimates the Effort Involved in a Project

1. Break down tasks into component parts and provide a checklist for each component. For example:
    *   Sometimes kids with planning difficulties avoid tasks because they don't know where to start. Planning out the project with a clear first step paves the way for them to get started.
    *   Work with the child to create a very specific list of the steps needed to complete the project. Consider together when each step needs to be done. For example, to lay out the process of cleaning his bedroom, you would start by listing the specific tasks. When will each step be completed? If company is scheduled to arrive on Wednesday, then the deadline is probably Tuesday evening. For a school project, divide the tasks into daily chunks, and enter these on the calendar or in an agenda book as homework. Remember to build in an extra day or two

for the unexpected so that your child gets into the habit of planning a cushion of extra time.

- Create picture lists for young children by drawing each step or cutting out pictures from magazines. For children that need a lot of support, particularly in the early stages of learning how to complete a task, such as teethbrushing, consider breaking the task into very small steps using systematic task analysis. Using photographs of the child doing the task can also be helpful.

2. Walk through the process with the child.
   - Review the assignment with your child and model the planning process by talking it through out loud. By verbalizing the steps you go through to plan and organize a task, you are teaching the process to the child. As your child gets older and/or shows you he is capable, you should switch to having the child lay out the plan. You can take a coaching role, helping the child only as much as is needed. Older children, or those whose parents are not well organized themselves, may benefit from working with a tutor who is skilled at helping those with executive skills deficits.

TIP: When complex projects or long-term papers are first assigned, it is helpful to emphasize the importance of planning by starting with a "planning day." The work on the project, itself, does not start on that day. Instead, on the planning day, the child's only task is to lay out the steps, determine needed materials, and develop the timeline for completing the project. This applies to studying for cumulative tests, as well. Creating a study plan is the first day's work.

3. Teach the use of tricks and technology that help to compensate for organizational weaknesses. For example:
   - Visual maps, either hand-written or created on a computer, are helpful for many people. Visual mapping programs allow the user to brainstorm and organize ideas in a visual format. The software can convert the visual format to outline form with the press of a button. Commonly used programs include Inspiration®, Kidspiration®, and Mindjet MindManager®.

(See Figure 15.1 on the next page.) For planning out the time and effort involved in long-term projects most kids do well to keep themselves on schedule by using an agenda book, wall calendar, or a white board. Remember, these tools only work if the child also has a habit to look at the planner, calendar, etc. on a regular basis. Until that habit is firmly established, he will need prompting to check the plan. There is no right way to keep organized. Whatever works for your child is the right system! The goal is to help the child maintain an overall vision of the plan for the project.

4. Develop templates for repetitive procedures. For example:
   - Create a template that can be used to guide the work each time. For example, you can use an index card to create a chore card that lists the steps to be completed for each chore, as Dr. Russell Barkley has suggested. A "kitchen clean-up" card might list the following tasks:
     1. Clear table of food and dishes
     2. Store leftovers in the refrigerator
     3. Load dirty dishes into dishwasher
     4. Wipe down table and countertops

5. Provide accommodations at home and at school. For example:
   - In some classrooms, it is common for teachers to provide a packet of information about each upcoming project. These often include a checklist of the steps and when each step is due. If this is not done as part of the normal classroom routine, request it as an accommodation for your child's formal or informal plan to address his individual weaknesses.
   - Ask your child's teachers for very specific instructions for your child, including exactly what is expected and when it is due. Ask for a list of all steps to be done to complete the project, specific expectations for each phase of the work, and due dates for each task. If asked, many teachers are willing to review the work along the way, as each step is due, to be sure that the student is on track.
   - For older students, a first step in the planning process might be to meet with the teacher to clarify expectations and timelines. Learning to ask for appropriate support is a critical skill that can make the difference between success and failure.

Figure 15.1

Mindjet MindManager Map

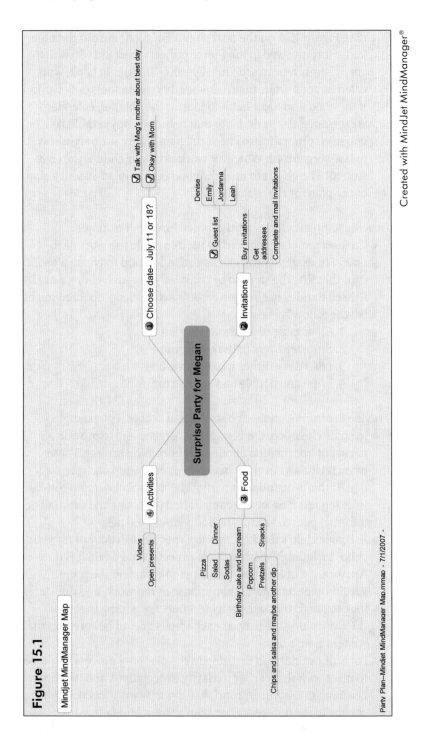

Surprise Party for Megan

① Choose date- July 11 or 18?
- ☑ Talk with Meg's mother about best day
- ☑ Okay with Mom

② Invitations
- ☑ Guest list
  - Denise
  - Emily
  - Jordanna
  - Leah
- Buy invitations
- Get addresses
- Complete and mail invitations

④ Activities
- Videos
- Open presents

③ Food
- Dinner
  - Pizza
  - Salad
  - Sodas
- Birthday cake and ice cream
- Snacks
  - Popcorn
  - Pretzels
  - Chips and salsa and maybe another dip

Party Plan—Mindjet MindManager Map.mmap - 7/1/2007 -

Created with MindJet MindManager®

Strategies to Help a Child Who Gets Overwhelmed by Juggling Several Classes or Projects at the Same Time

1. Break down tasks into component parts and provide a checklist for each component.
   - Arrange a specific time daily to review tasks with your child and to consider together what things need to be accomplished. Outline the various areas of responsibility, activities, chores, and whatever else needs your child's attention. Help your child to break down each area into a step-by-step list. Consider together when each step needs to be done.

2. Teach the use of tricks and technology that help to compensate for organizational weaknesses. For example:
   - The same visual organizers and mind-mapping software that helps students to organize a paper or project can help with tracking various projects at once. These visual mapping programs allow the user to organize the whole range of projects in a visual format. The software can convert the visual format to outline form with the press of a button. By mapping out the task, the student is pushed to consider what is required for each step.

TIP: Technology provides great prospects for helping those who are poorly organized. These tools contain the seeds of independence, but once they are learned they must be used repeatedly before they become habits. Short-term interventions involve teaching the child to use the tool and working with the child as he practices. Once the child is able to use the technology, your role is to monitor its use and to prompt the child if he is not habitually taking advantage of the technology independently. Be flexible in adapting the use of technology and considering new tools as they come on the market. As with so many interventions, this is a trial and error process. If it works or has good potential to work, keep at it. If it does not meet your child's needs or suit his style, perhaps there is something else that may work better.

3. Provide accommodations at home and at school. For example:
   - Simplify your child's schedule at home. Consider reducing the number of extra-curricular activities, allowing your child to focus on those things that are most important and enjoyable to him.
   - For high school and college students, sometimes it just makes more sense to reduce the course load and plan to take one or two courses during the summer or simply adopt the five (or six) year plan. Bright students with executive weaknesses often find that they can ace just about any class if they take only the one class at a time. It is the juggling of many classes at once that is difficult.
   - Recognize that children may not always shine, despite native abilities! Teach children to consider the relative importance of the various expectations they are facing. For example, if service to the community is important to your family, then you and your child may decide that he will put in less homework time over the weekend and accept the risk of a lower grade on Monday's test in order to spend time on a Habitat for Humanity project over the weekend.
   - Ask for a syllabus or advance notice of upcoming assignments. This allows you and your child to identify the most demanding times of the week or semester so that appropriate adjustments can be made in the homework/study schedule.

Strategies to Help a Student Determine the Most Important Information from Material to Be Learned

1. Offer organizational frameworks in advance that help students organize new material in their heads. For example:
   - Discuss the most important points to be learned before the child starts an independent reading task. In educational language, this is known as previewing the lesson. ("You are going to read about the Civil War. This chapter focuses on the personal side of what it was like during that time. I want you to notice what people wore and what they ate on the farms and in the cities, how families managed at home when most of the able men were away, and what life was like for the men fighting the war.")

- Provide an outline of the major topics and sub-topics from the text with space for the student to fill in specific information as he reads.
- Offer study questions in advance so that the student understands the learning objectives before beginning to read.

2. Teach the use of tricks and technology that help to compensate for organizational weaknesses. For example:
    - Teach the student to highlight or underline the most important words in the directions and the most important information in a paragraph or chapter.
    - Teach the student to orient himself before reading a chapter by first reading the questions at the end of the chapter. In this way, the child can more easily recognize the most important information in the chapter as he reads it.
    - Teach a student to write a one sentence summary on a sticky-note after reading each paragraph. This promotes comprehension and produces an outline.

TRY THIS!

One very effective tutor teaches her students to build a framework for new material by using the layout of the chapter. She teaches students to sit at their computers with their textbooks and to type in all the chapter headings and subheadings before starting their reading. This becomes both a concrete outline for taking notes and an internal framework upon which to hang the details of the material. Some students fill in the details as they are reading, while others do better if they go back and take more specific notes after reading through the whole chapter.

3. Provide accommodations at home and at school.
    - All of the techniques described above can be requested as school accommodations on formal or informal educational plans.
    - Preview important discussions with your child or teen. For example, when you initiate a family meeting, preview and categorize the information you need to discuss. "Sammy, we need to sit down together this evening to plan the things you

need to get done before we go on vacation. We talked about some chores and also one summer reading project that you need to get done over the next two months. You may have some other things to add to the list. Let's review and plan after dinner tonight."

Strategies to Help a Child Organize His Backpack (and Locker, Desk, Bedroom, etc.)

1. Walk through the process with the child.
   - Consider together how and when materials need to be organized. Talk through each step of the process and find out where the process is breaking down. Then consider what steps need to be added or changed for the child to be more successful.

2. Offer organizational frameworks in advance.
   - Define what the organized space should look like. Where does each thing go? What belongs in a backpack or desk? Where do the other things belong? While it helps to talk a child through how you are organizing something as you are doing it, visual supports are also a very effective tool. Sometimes providing your child with a photograph of an organized desk or all the items that typically belong in his backpack can help him get a better grasp of what it means to be organized.

3. Provide accommodations at home and at school. For example:
   - Provide frequent monitoring and help with organizing materials. Hands-on help is often needed for younger children. For older children and for those who show that they are capable of more independent functioning, back off of direct help but provide frequent checks to ensure that the space is not getting out of control.
   - Some children need to have a scheduled time to organize their materials. For example, they may need to clean their desks or lockers every Friday and use some weekend time to sort all the papers and items they clear out. A daily or weekly backpack cleaning is often helpful, as well.

TIPS: Remember to prioritize the goals for organization. Although a messy room may drive you crazy, it may serve the child better in the long run to help him develop a system to get long-term projects done on time.

Don't assume that a child knows how to organize a backpack, notebook, or locker. Talk to the child about organizational methods that might work for him and let him watch you clean out your kitchen junk drawer!

CASE STUDY: PUTTING IT ALL TOGETHER

Let us introduce you to Jim. He tends to wait until the last minute to start papers and projects, generally stating (and believing!) that the work will be "no big deal" and won't take long. He seems genuinely surprised each time he discovers anew that starting work the night before an assignment is due does not allow enough time to get all the work done. Like many students, Jim has become more discouraged over the years. Now in eighth grade, he tends to respond to his difficulties by giving up or pretending that he doesn't care. While most of the adults in his life focus on his less than stellar effort, Jim's new Language Arts teacher has helped his parents to see that Jim has developmental delays in his ability to independently plan and organize his assignments, belongings, and even his thoughts. While Jim managed to do okay in elementary school, he is having significant difficulty in middle school. And his parents are very worried about what's in store for all of them when Jim gets to high school.

Jim's planning and organizational deficits are complicated by his feelings of demoralization and his tendency to give up when he gets frustrated. With their new insight into his seeming lack of motivation, thanks to an astute teacher, his parents and the school have recently initiated interventions to help Jim learn to organize and plan his work. Despite the fact that Jim is in the eighth grade

(continued on next page)

(continued from previous page)

and in theory should be able to do this on his own, Jim's parents have gone back to providing a higher level of external structure and organizational support, as they did for him when he was younger. They review his assignments with him and help break them down into component parts with checklists for him to follow. They have acquired a software program for mapping out tasks, and they are learning together how to use it.

At school, teachers provide specific timelines for the components of long-term projects to help guide Jim in his planning. They set interim due dates to keep him on track. Jim is starting to understand his own difficulty, and so he is feeling more hopeful about being able to do well at school. His parents are trying to carefully balance out their roles as they offer help but strive to do so in a manner that is developmentally appropriate and does not promote learned helplessness or over-dependence. Now there's a challenge!

Transitioning From Short-Term to Long-Term Goals

The goal of your interventions as you help your child with planning and organizing is to create systems that become habitual and to give your child a repertoire of ways to approach a task. Short-term interventions are those that create the structure for your child. You are providing this support so that your child can meet expectations while you use the tasks of daily life to teach him how to plan and organize. As he matures and his proficiency increases, you ease up on the support. However, the objective is clear from the outset: you are teaching him ways to independently manage demands.

Teachers will recognize an important teaching approach here known as scaffolding. While the content is not social studies or language arts, the process of teaching planning and organizational skills at school or at home is the same. Just as with any other content area, the student will need instruction, practice, and feedback until he accumulates sufficient knowledge and experience to build up some momentum and take off on his own. One experience builds on another over time, and the skills he has learned work together in such a way that the scaffolding can be removed and the building stands on its own. However, with disorganized kids, you should expect that there will be a tendency to revert back to disorganized mode, at times. Your monitoring, or perhaps monitoring by a tutor or coach, will be important for a long time.

Educate Others and Advocate For Your Child

Planning and organization are essential for efficient task completion and management. Being able to determine how to organize information without outside help is essential to academic success and to establishing an efficient daily routine. When kids struggle with these skills, they need direct, intensive help to develop successful habits.

Remember, the goal is not to promote overdependence or learned helplessness. Such problems may occur when parents and other important adults complete tasks *for* rather than *with* the child and when they continue to provide more support than needed. Children and adolescents only develop more effective planning and organizational skills through maturation and experience. No amount of wishing, lecturing, prodding, or punishment leads to skill development. If your child is generally putting forth adequate effort, one of the most useful ways you can help him is to help teachers and others understand that his disorganization is not due to a moral flaw or lack of interest in performing well.

Help for your child can take a variety of forms. Some schools, public and private, focus a great deal of effort on teaching organizational skills. Find out what your child's school can offer. Be sure to look at the ways that your child will be taught the skills for independence, not just how his weaknesses will be accommodated. If your child's school does not already require teachers to post assignments and test dates on the school website, you may want to advocate for this through the PTA or by talking with administrators. There are now many types of software programs and technology applications that are extremely helpful for disorganized kids. For example, some schools require teachers to record grades online as well as missing or incomplete assignments. Parents and students are provided with access to this information so that appropriate supports can be put in place before a student begins performing poorly.

While we have also seen some well-organized parents do a remarkable job of supporting and teaching their own children and adolescents, you may need to seek a tutor or coach who understands the process well.

Final Thoughts

Kids are not always thrilled about putting in the time that is required to develop improved planning and organization skills. How much and how far you can coax, push, and/or lead a child is not something that is clearly defined. There is no research here to guide us. Hopefully, as the steps become routine and the child or teen experiences success, the resistance will diminish.

Remember, these skills can be learned through a variety of ways, not just schoolwork. Some parents cut off all outside activities, with the intention of pushing the child to focus on school and so perform better. Instead, we recommend that you work with your child to pick the one or two extracurricular activities that put a spring in your child's step, and then use these as training grounds for planning and organization skills, too. In fact, many disorganized kids do best when their day includes a reasonable balance between school and outside activities.

16

Helping Children Monitor Their Behavior

Self-Monitoring = The ability to observe one's own behavior and track progress toward a goal.

Self-monitoring can be viewed as the brain's quality control system. The ability to step back and observe one's own behavior is essential to social competence and school success. Kids with weak self-monitoring ability tend to be oblivious regarding their own behavior and whether or not they are meeting behavioral standards until they receive external appraisal. Additionally, they tend to misjudge their own efforts toward goals. They have difficulty taking in feedback from the environment and using it to adjust their behavioral or work performance. Despite clues along the way, these kids often find that negative evaluations of their work or their behavior come as a total surprise.

When a child isn't able to monitor how she is doing, it's difficult for her to learn from previous experiences, and adapt her future behavior accordingly. Simply put, if she doesn't know what she did to irritate her classmate on the playground, how can she avoid doing it again next time?

In academics, poor self-monitoring is particularly apparent in math and writing. Students with weaknesses in this executive skill tend to make seemingly careless computation errors and have trouble proofreading their written work.

Successful self-monitoring is much like driving a car. It seems effortless when it is going well. Yet when we drive, we are constantly engaged in monitoring our behavior, the environmental conditions, and the interplay between the two. We adjust our driving speed or make minor course corrections without conscious effort. However, if you think back to when you first learned to drive, you may remember how complex and effortful the task seemed. As opposed to the amount of effort required for beginning drivers, experienced drivers automatically complete these monitoring functions and only have to think about how they are doing when they are fatigued or encounter unexpected events (e.g., a car pulling out in front of us).

Interventions for children with self-monitoring weaknesses are designed to help them to develop routines for checking their work, for comparing their own behavior to a standard, and for tuning into environmental feedback. With repetition, these may become automatic, even though they will require self-conscious effort at the start.

You may notice that there are fewer examples of interventions in this chapter than appear in the previous intervention chapters. The problems arising from weak self-monitoring and the solutions for dealing with them overlap a great deal with the interventions for problems with other executive skills. After all, the long-term goal for all executive weaknesses is to help children to understand their own behavior and to know what to do to help navigate the problems. So, building self-awareness and self-observation is part of the interventions we have presented in earlier chapters. We offer some interventions specific to self-monitoring in this chapter. However, if your child has difficulties with self-monitoring, you might want to read through the recommendations for other executive skills to get more ideas of how to help.

Strategies reviewed in this chapter help children who:

- don't notice when they have gone off on a tangent;
- don't notice when they make seemingly "careless" errors;
- fail to adjust behavior based on feedback;
- don't notice when peers are no longer interested in the topic of conversation; and
- are genuinely surprised when they get in trouble for misbehavior ("What did I do?")

Below, we've listed general intervention strategies that you'll want to employ with your child who has difficulty monitoring her behavior. Further down, we've provided advice for dealing with more specific scenarios that you're likely to experience with your child or teen. Note that depending on the issue you are addressing with your child, you will typically use only a subset of the strategies discussed in this chapter.

> ## SUMMARY: GENERAL STRATEGIES TO HELP YOUR CHILD LEARN HOW TO SELF-MONITOR
>
> **Provide external structure and feedback.** This needs to be done in a sensitive, developmentally appropriate manner.
>
> **Teach the use of tools and techniques to improve monitoring,** including checklists for repetitive tasks.
>
> **Highlight the process of self-review and analysis of behavior.** Many children with these weaknesses don't engage in the crucial step of analyzing their past failures in order to improve future performance.
>
> **Teach the use of technology** to help the child monitor her performance.

Strategies to Help a Child Who Doesn't Notice When She Has Gone Off on a Tangent

1. Provide external structure and feedback. For example:
   - Monitor the child's performance along the way and prompt the child to go back to the topic and re-focus. For example:
     ➤ "Remember, the goal of this paper is to present one side of a controversial argument. Do these points support your position?"
     ➤ "You certainly know a lot about the Civil War. Let's focus on this specific question, though. Can you tell us the three most important events of the Battle of Gettysburg?"
     ➤ "Eli, I'm so glad you enjoyed the new video game. I know you have a lot you would like to say about it. But we need to focus now on the plans for today and who you would like to invite to go to the pool with us."
     ➤ "Peter, you have done an amazing job describing your year for the family holiday letter. So, you have finished

Helping Children Monitor Their Behavior

part of the job. Can you please now include what has happened for your sister, father, and me?"

- Provide a rubric that lays out clear evaluation criteria and prompt the child to refer back to it. Rubrics are checklists that delineate what the child will be graded on and how many points of the total grade will be allotted for each of the things on the list.

2. Teach the use of tools and techniques to improve monitoring. For example:

- Teach the student to re-read the directions to be certain she is on topic.
- Work with the student to develop an outline before she begins writing, and prompt her to check the outline after writing each section.
- For students who often miss information during class lectures, provide an outline or organizer for the student to complete as she is listening. Teach children to review the outline to be certain that they have information in all of the sections as a way of determining whether or not they have taken complete notes.

TIP: When it is time for your child to clean her room, don't assume that she knows all of the necessary steps. Be prepared to break down the task into reasonable steps and to show her what needs to be done. Some kids do fine with verbal prompts while others need very specific direction and a checklist so they can evaluate whether or not they're done. Chore cards, introduced in Chapter 14, work well in this regard.

Strategies to Help a Child Who Doesn't Notice "Careless" Errors

1. Provide external structure and feedback. For example:

- Make the evaluation criteria explicit. For example:
  ➤ "You will lose points if you have not put your name on the paper or have skipped any questions. Remember, name on the paper and all questions answered."
  ➤ "The assignment sheet says that you will be graded on the presentation of the material, including the design and

appearance of the cover. That means that the cover page should be clean, neat, and have an interesting design that reflects what your paper is about. I do not want to see erasures and hand-written corrections. If you have made corrections, you should print out a new, corrected copy of the cover page."

➤ "If you have cleaned up after you made yourself a snack, I should not be able to tell what you had to eat or even that you made a snack at all. Make sure that you have cleaned up your trail. That includes using a sponge to wipe up the little spills near the microwave and the crumbs on the counter."

• Prompt the child to check her work against the standard. For example:

➤ About ten minutes before the exam or in-class assignment is due, the teacher can make a quick announcement: "Please go to the first page, make sure your name is on your paper and then check to make sure you haven't skipped any questions." If your child has an IEP or 504 Plan, you may want to consider adding this support, which does not adversely affect her peers and may, in fact, be helpful to some of them.

➤ Work with children to help them re-check their own performance on papers and projects assigned as homework. "Deanna, let's take a look at the checklist to see if you have all the pieces that your teacher is expecting."

➤ "Before I come upstairs to look at your room, I want you to go back up and check it yourself. I want you to stand at the door, and this time pretend you are the parent. See if you think the work is all done."

➤ "Tina, you did a great job loading the dishwasher. Now, I see one more thing you need to do. Do you see it? Just wipe off the counter above the dishwasher, and then your work is done and you can have some free time."

2. Teach the use of tools and techniques to improve self-monitoring. For example:

• For math computation, teach the student to highlight or circle math operation signs.

- Teach the student to say each math calculation problem aloud so that she is less likely to miss the operation sign.
- Direct the student to use a specific copy editing procedure (e.g., circle misspellings, underline punctuation/capitalization errors).
- For brief written work, teach the student to proofread by reading the last sentence first and then progressing backwards to the beginning. This breaks up the context and allows the mistakes to stand out.
- Develop a work routine and have your child practice it until it becomes automatic. For example, Sierra's grandmother practiced the following with her:
    1. Read the directions out loud
    2. Underline key words (e.g., not, all, if)
    3. Re-read the directions after completing your answer, and ask yourself, "Did I answer the question?"
- Walk through a "guesstimate" procedure for math problems. Ask the student to estimate the answer and to take an educated guess about whether the answer is likely to be correct. ("Do you think the answer will be less or greater than ten?" "Let's see, the problem talks about how many cookies the girl ate. Your answer is 3,500. Does that sound reasonable?")
- If the assignment packet includes a rubric to help the students determine how they will be graded, coach children to refer back to it at each step of the project and then to grade themselves before pronouncing the work complete.
- Ask your child to estimate how long it takes to complete a task. For example, ask her to guess how long it will take to pack her lunch and backpack. Write down her estimate and then time her.

3. Teach the use of technology to help a student self-monitor. For example:
    - Coach students to use the spell-check feature of their word processing software.
    - Provide word prediction software for weaker spellers. (These programs take the first few letters as a student begins typing a word, and offer a list of possible words based on the beginning.)
    - Encourage the use of writing software (such as Inspiration® or Don Johnston's CoWriter®) to generate outlines and review written work. These and other programs provide templates

for different types of writing. Once a student has completed a draft, the student can use the template to check if the paper contains all needed parts.

TIP: When you provide feedback on a child's behavior, it is important to stick to observations of the child's behavior and to avoid "riders," added-on comments that exact an emotional price. Riders carry a negative tone that overrides any other content in the message. Here is an example of two different parental responses to the same behavior, the first includes riders and the second doesn't. "Ellen, you left your dishes on the table again. I don't know how many times I've told you not to do that! Why are you such a slob? Don't you care about how this place looks?" Or, "Ellen, you left your dishes on the table. This seems to be a recurring problem. Can you think of anything we might be able to do to help you remember to tidy up the kitchen when you make yourself a snack?" Which one do you think is likely to be most effective? If you can clean up your messages to remove the negative tone, you will likely find that your child is more receptive to your feedback and suggestions.

Strategies to Help a Child Who Fails to Adjust Behavior Based on Feedback

1. Highlight the process of self-review and analysis of behavior. For example:
   - Encourage the child to analyze past incidents in order to improve her ability to think about behavior. ("Kenya, the last time we were at the playground, you pushed a little girl down the slide. I realize you thought she would enjoy it, but she didn't. Please stop to think before you act while you're playing today.")
   - When the child is calm, ask her to generate other ways to handle a problem or specific situation. Ask the child to list possible consequences of each option. ("I know that your sleepover with Tracy didn't turn out like you wanted. Let's talk about what you could've done differently to prevent the argument.")
   - When possible, stop the action and help the child analyze her own behavior. Then do a replay incorporating more effective

behaviors. Remember to incorporate a brief discussion of what she *should* do, not just what the child did wrong. ("Serena, hold on here for just a minute. I heard Mary say that she did not want you sitting so close to her. What do you think you should do? That's a good idea. Let's see how that works.")

TIP: Teaching social skills to children is more complex and often less effective than you might think. If these general interventions are not helpful, you should seek consultation from a professional who is well-versed in interventions for social skills deficits. While a full overview of how to approach social skills problems is outside the scope of this book, research in this area suggests that the best outcomes occur when social behavior is taught in natural settings, when behaviors are carefully assessed in advance, when each child's specific deficits are targeted, and when transfer from the teaching environment to real life is part of the work.

Strategies to Help a Child Notice When Peers Are No Longer Interested in the Topic of Conversation

1. Provide external structure and feedback. For example:
   - "Leah, when you talk about your favorite TV show, you sometimes say more than the other kids want to hear. So I want you to keep your talk about that to three sentences. No more than three sentences on that topic. Got it?"
   - "Sheila, when I walked in the room, I could see you over there with two other girls. It looked to me like they turned away when you said something to them. Did you notice that? That probably means that they did not want to talk with you."
   - "Let's talk about what happened on the school trip. James apparently got tired of you talking about your trip to the zoo. He tried to change the subject a few times. Do you remember what he said?"
   - "Cindy kept trying to talk with you about the prom while you kept talking about math class. I think her facial expression was a clue that she was no longer interested."

2. Teach the use of tools and techniques to improve monitoring, including checklists for repetitive tasks. For example:
   - Teach and practice reading body language in social interactions. How can you tell, even without words, whether someone is bored or interested in what you are saying? Make a list together of different ways someone might indicate boredom and review it when you are "re-playing" where things go wrong in social interchanges.
   - Sarah's school counselor has worked with her teachers to help her slow down and read the facial expression of the person she is talking to. When that doesn't give her enough information about whether or not she is being clear in her conversation, Sarah has learned to directly ask the other person if she has been talking too long or if she is making sense.

Strategies to Help a Child Who is Genuinely Surprised When She Gets in Trouble for Misbehavior ("What Did I Do?")

1. Provide external support and feedback. For example:
   - Pat is a bright twelve-year-old who has trouble anticipating the consequences for her behavior. Even though her P.E. teacher blew the warning whistle three times, she was surprised when she got pulled from the soccer game for being too rough. Once she calmed down, her teacher agreed to stay close to her on the sidelines and remind her to keep her hands to herself, since the whistle didn't seem to help her keep track of how she was doing.

2. Encourage the child to analyze past behavior in order to improve self-monitoring. For example:
   - "Jon, I know you were surprised when your Sunday school teacher asked you to leave the class because you were talking. Sometimes it is hard to know when you are talking too much. Maybe we should talk with her to find some clues to figure this out. They might include how she looks at you, what she says, and what other kids are doing. I know you don't want to get in trouble and it is important to be able to figure out how to prevent this from happening in the future."

CASE STUDY: PUTTING IT ALL TOGETHER

Luis is a fifth grader who struggles with self-monitoring. Although he is bright and wants to do well, he often skips test questions, not noticing that he has blanks on the answer sheet. He only sees his errors when the test is returned with vivid red X's marking the overlooked test questions. His efforts are sometimes misplaced. For example, he may spend a lot of time on the first step of a class project, oblivious to the fact that his classmates are nearly ready to turn theirs in. Luis tends to spend a long time completing homework, but he doesn't catch mistakes, particularly when he perceives the task as easy. When completing a chore such as taking out the trash, he may not notice that he has dropped items or that the top of the garbage can is not latched. It is only when his father tells him the next morning that the squirrels helped themselves to leftovers (and made quite a mess) that he becomes aware that his performance was not quite up to standard.

Luis' parents and teachers have become quite frustrated with his inconsistent performance and frequent missteps. They have tried punishing Luis, lecturing him, and reminding him to be more careful. Nothing seems to help. Luis is as frustrated as the adults. He is also quite discouraged. He sometimes talks about feeling stupid, most recently when he mistakenly thought that he did great on a project and then got a low grade due to an overlooked part of the assignment.

His parents have become increasingly concerned about his loss of self-confidence and waning self-esteem. They've decided to take him to a psychologist for a few sessions to learn more about self-monitoring and other executive skills so that he will understand that his difficulties are not due to poor motivation or a lack of intelligence. Although this may not be appropriate for all ten-year-olds, Luis's cognitive and personality profile are such that learning more is important before enlisting his cooperation in deciding how best to manage these weaknesses.

Luis and his parents have since worked out a system where they edit and check his work much like a copy editor does for a professional writer (e.g., purple marks indicate a need to check spelling, orange is used for punctuation and capitalization, and green marks the need to review or rework the whole problem or sentence). Instead of standing over him while making corrections, Luis hands in his work and they review it and mark omissions and errors while he works on other tasks. Twice a week, Luis also works with a tutor/coach in his home. The tutor is helping him experiment with ways to improve his self-monitoring. So far, he has learned that proofreading aloud works quite well for him (he is a strong reader), and he is learning how to more effectively use the spell- and grammar-check features when word processing. Luis and his tutor are also experimenting with a checklist to help him consistently re-read directions to ensure that he has done what he was asked to do.

Luis and his parents have met with all of his teachers and agreed that each will check in with him fifteen minutes before the end of any quiz or test. If there are blank sections or questions, they point this out in a sensitive manner to give him time to complete the work. Some of his teachers have found that taking thirty seconds to make this double check announcement to the whole class has benefited other students as well. In addition, Luis' math teacher allows him to use a calculator to double check his computations on tests.

When completing chores at home, Luis's parents remind him to do a visual inspection after the job is done and, when appropriate, do this with him. If a part of the job is not completed, they acknowledge his good effort and gently prompt him to finish what needs to be done.

Transitioning from Short-Term to Long-Term Goals

As parents and teachers, we aim to help kids learn how to keep better track of how they are doing. Providing external cues, prompts, and feedback helps children learn what to watch out for and how often to check how they are doing. We begin by staying physically close to the child and providing frequent verbal and nonverbal cues. For example, we ensure that she is brushing her teeth adequately by standing next to her and watching while she brushes. Next, we leave the room briefly while she brushes and offer verbal reinforcement from the next room. Then, we may have her brush independently daily and use a plaque-detecting rinse once a week that shows any missed areas by turning the plaque a bright color. When she is consistently doing a good job we may drop out the weekly rinse entirely, reviving it only occasionally when we think she is slipping.

As with other areas of executive function, we need to teach the child or teen about her own profile in a straightforward, nonjudgmental manner and then teach her the tricks and systems that will help her to monitor her own work more accurately. We back away from active involvement as the child or teen's own self-monitoring system improves, and move to just prompting the use of strategies that she has been taught. When we see her begin to initiate strategies on her own, we support her independence by offering praise for using what she has learned.

Our long-term goal is to help children develop a sufficient internal quality control system so that external monitoring is greatly reduced or no longer needed. We are looking for evidence that the process of self-monitoring is becoming more automatic and less effortful over time. When self-monitoring remains relatively weak, it is important for adolescents (and adults) to learn to enlist the help of others to provide feedback and support.

Educate Others and Advocate for Your Child

Kids who struggle with self-monitoring often demonstrate inconsistent performance and are prone to "careless" errors. Parents should talk with teachers to help them understand that such mistakes are not related to a lack of motivation but, instead, to developmental weaknesses in quality control. Since kids with certain temperaments attempt to manage self-monitoring problems by pretending not to care about their performance, we sometimes need to help teachers, coaches, and other important adults understand the need to look beyond a child's "surface" presentation to provide an appropriate level of assistance. And although it is tempting, no amount of lecturing ("It is important to work carefully.") has ever been an effective intervention.

Weak self-monitoring often occurs in combination with impulsiveness and poor regulation of attention. Teachers often encounter this cluster of behaviors and may have some good ideas to share. Both at home and at school, it is essential to provide these supports in a noncritical manner. Just as every best-selling author has a great editor, our kids with limited self-monitoring skills may need to have their work reviewed by a trusted adult.

Final Thoughts

As noted above, children who have trouble with self-monitoring are generally impulsive, as well. For a child to determine how she is doing, she must first slow down enough to think and review. Many of the interventions to reduce impulsive behavior are also useful for improving self-monitoring. Efficient self-monitoring also requires adequate attention and developing habits and routines for regularly checking how one is doing. It is a complex behavior; however, it is an important behavioral target. By helping children and adolescents to develop better self-monitoring, we hope to reduce their risk for academic underachievement, inconsistent school performance, and social problems.

17

Concluding Thoughts

Raising a child with executive weaknesses requires patience, flexibility, humor, and creativity. Out of synch with developmental expectations, your child faces situations wherein routine demands put him at risk for inconsistent performance at best, or failure at worst. We hope the knowledge you have acquired from this book about the nature of executive skills and possible interventions gives direction to your efforts to help your child succeed.

The Zen of Intervention Planning

The goal of interventions is to help our children to extend their abilities, one small step at a time, by working right at the edge of what they can do now and helping them move on to the next step. This requires an ongoing evaluation process as maturation occurs, as learning and experience move our children forward, and as expectations change.

So we must continually re-evaluate our own efforts. Are we doing too much? Are we doing enough? Do we need to experiment with different ways of providing support?

Maintaining the delicate balance between support and skill building is essential to promoting healthy development. If we only accommodate executive weaknesses without attempting to strengthen them, we may be promoting dependency and helplessness. However, if we expect our children to develop these skills without appropriate accommodations, it is unlikely that they will succeed. In the face of repeated inability to meet expectations, children get overwhelmed and become demoralized. So, we want to offer appropriate levels of support and accommodation.

However, just to make adults' jobs even more complex, we need to reiterate here that one of the most challenging aspects of raising a child with executive dysfunction is dealing with the inconsistency that characterizes his performance. On some days, in some situations, on some tasks, your child may perform beautifully. However, even on a similar task, on a different day, your child may struggle. In our clinical work, we have developed an appreciation for how this variability confounds children and adults, alike.

Now for some good news! As complex as this all sounds, this is a job that we have seen done well over and over again. Parents with whom we have worked have demonstrated remarkable grace and wisdom, even as they fly by the seat of their pants. It is our goal to ground you in specific knowledge to use as guideposts, so perhaps you are flying in a more determined direction.

However, there is no standard formula for parenting. Between the endpoints of doing too much and not doing enough, you find lots of variability. It is essential to regularly test the waters by fading supports and accommodations to see if your child has gained sufficient skills to manage tasks independently.

The "No Victims" Approach

We hope we have made it clear that we believe that kids who must operate in the world without the benefit of strong executive skills deserve our understanding and compassion. They got a bum deal on this one! However, it is the ability to accept and master one's own challenges in life that constitutes strong character. Understanding executive weaknesses provides an explanation for difficulties, not an excuse. By balancing support with skill building, we promote development in our children without giving them a free pass on expectations.

When we actively involve kids in determining what is getting in their way and thinking about how to get around their weaknesses, we promote an active, engaged approach to building success. We expect kids to get weary of the effort, at times, and we offer empathy as we listen to their inevitable frustration, anger, and sadness.

We also offer straightforward guidance, making it clear that they have to work harder than other kids in their areas of weakness, because the skills do not come naturally to them like they do for some others.

And as parents and professionals, we must help children identify and build on those things that *do* come naturally to them so that they can build a balanced view of themselves.

Building a Life

School difficulties, particularly, seem to knock families off balance. School is such an important focus of kids' lives and occupies such a large percentage of their time and efforts in the first two decades of life, that we sometimes lose perspective. We do not mean to dismiss its importance in any way. At the same time, however, school does not constitute a whole life.

We have seen some families in which the child's cumulative grade-point average appears to be the sole measure of his success. We encourage you to think more broadly about success. In so doing, you encourage your child to have a more balanced view, as well. Not all kids will shine in school, but they can be stars nonetheless.

Kids must be supported in their strengths, whatever those are. Is your child interested in drama? An enthusiastic dog lover? A natural at baseball? Provide opportunities for expanding these interests and experiencing real pleasure in the world by helping kids do what they do best. A child who is very compassionate might be just the person to make sandwiches for the local homeless shelter. A teen with great people skills might benefit from the skills and sense of competence he can build by working part-time at the local toy store.

Dr. Robert Brooks, a psychologist and author who has written about building resilience in children and adults with learning disabilities, describes the importance of helping people discover their islands of competence. "Many of these children and adults seem to be drowning in an ocean of self-perceived inadequacy....If there is an ocean of inadequacy, then there must be islands of competence—areas that have been or have the potential to be sources of pride and accomplishment." He goes on to explain the potential that lives on these islands. "If we can find and reinforce these areas of strength, we can create a powerful 'ripple effect' in which children and adults may be more willing to venture forth and confront situations that have been problematic." (*The Search for Islands of Competence: A Metaphor of Hope and Strength*, online monthly article, June, 2005.)

Similarly, Dr. Mel Levine, a pediatrician who has written many books for kids and adults on understanding learning differences, points out that we expect school-age kids to be "good at *everything*...math, reading, writing, speaking, spelling, memorization, comprehension, problem solving, socialization, athletics, and following verbal directions" (*A Mind at a Time*, Simon & Schuster, 2002). However, as adults, most of us gravitate to areas that tap our interests and abilities in the worlds of work and relationships.

Like Drs. Brooks and Levine, we believe that our children's best hope for the future may lay in the discovery of some strength that blossoms into an island of competence, and perhaps even becomes a continent of possibilities for personal satisfaction and job success. After all, people thrive when they build a life around their strengths. There are many different paths to success, even though this is sometimes hard to keep in perspective during the school years.

Who Can Help?

Teachers, sports coaches, and scout leaders all can have a role in helping your child develop better executive skills. Remember to pool all available informal resources. Whether or not the person has specific professional training, some folks have a marvelous intuitive sense of what a particular child needs in order to build competence and to be successful. However, in some cases, you may wish to seek the help of professionals.

Tutors can be very helpful for kids struggling to meet academic demands. When you enlist a tutor, seek one who uses the specific course content as an opportunity to work on the broader issues of task management, as well as working on the class material.

Organizational skills coaches and AD/HD coaches specialize in helping people define and meet specific behavioral goals. They generally work with older teens and adults.

Mental health professionals who specialize in working with children and families struggling with learning disabilities and AD/HD can be an invaluable resource, as well. They can counsel parents to help them understand and facilitate their child's development. At times, it can be helpful to have the therapist work individually with a child to help him understand his own strengths and weaknesses. Additionally, a mental health professional can help if your child is suffering from some of the secondary problems associated with executive issues, including frustration, anxiety, and depression.

A Field in Progress

The study of brain functioning, in general, and executive skills, specifically, is an active and exciting arena. Our understanding of both typical and atypical brain development is growing through basic research and advances in technology that allow scientists to watch the brain at work. We look forward to new understandings as the field advances, and know that we will continue to advance our knowledge of how to help those with executive weaknesses.

Our clinical experiences provide a different source of learning. On an almost daily basis, we hear from children, parents, and teachers about what works for them and what does not. We know that there is no "one size fits all" approach and that we need to consider each child's personality, environment, and cognitive profile in order to design the most effective interventions. We look forward to hearing from those of you who are on the front lines, and hope that you will contact us with your ideas so that we can learn from you.

We wish you strength, good humor, grace, and joy in your parenting. We hope that this book helps you in your efforts.

Appendix

Below are some examples of tests that tap various aspects of executive functioning in children and adolescents. Remember that no single test constitutes an assessment of executive functioning. The results of any test must be put into a meaningful context by looking at how the child does on a variety of different types of measures and in daily life.

Single Tests

California Verbal Learning Test-Children's Version (CVLT-C)
California Verbal Learning Test-Second Edition (CVLT-II)
Category Test (Halstead-Reitan)
Children's Category Test
Controlled Oral Word Association (verbal fluency)
Rey-Osterrieth Complex Figure Test
Stroop Color and Word Test
Tower of London ^{DX} 2nd Edition
Trail Making Test (Halstead-Reitan)
Wisconsin Card Sorting Test

Test Batteries

Behavioural Assessment of the Dysexecutive Syndrome
     for Children
Das-Naglieri Cognitive Assessment System (CAS)
Delis-Kaplan Executive Function System (D-KEFS)
NEPSY Second Edition (NEPSY-II)
Neuropsychological Assessment Battery
Test of Everyday Attention for Children (TEA-Ch)

Continuous Performance Tests (assess attention and impulse control)

Conners' Continuous Performance Test II

Gordon Diagnostic System

Integrated Visual & Auditory Continuous Performance
Test (IVA)

Test of Variables of Attention (TOVA)

Rating Scales

Behavior Rating Inventory of Executive Function (BRIEF)

Behavior Assessment System for Children and Adolescents-
Second Edition (BASC-2)

Brown ADD Scales

Conners Third Edition

References

American Psychiatric Association. *Diagnostic and Statistical Manual of Mental Disorders DSM-IV-TR (Text Revision)*. Arlington, VA: American Psychiatric Publishing, Inc., 2000.

Anderson, Peter. "Assessment and Development of Executive Function (EF) During Childhood." *Child Neuropsychology, 8(2)* (2002), 71-823.

Anderson, Stephen. *Self-Help Skills for People with Autism: A Systematic Teaching Approach*. Bethesda, MD: Woodbine House, 2007.

Anderson, Vicki. "Assessing Executive Functions in Children: Biological, Psychological, and Developmental Considerations. *Neuropsychological Rehabilitation, 8(3)* (1998), 319-349.

Anderson, Winifred, Stephen R. Chitwood, Deidre Hayden, Cherie Takemoto. *Negotiating the Special Education Maze: A Guide for Parents and Teachers, 4th ed*. Bethesda, MD: Woodbine House, 2008.

Barkley, Russell A. *ADHD and the Nature of Self-Control*. New York, NY: Guilford Press, 2005.

Barkley, Russell A. *Attention-Deficit Hyperactivity Disorder: A Handbook for Diagnosis and Treatment, 3rd ed*. New York, NY: Guilford Press, 2006.

Barkley, Russell A. *Defiant Children: A Clinician's Manual for Assessment and Parent Training*. New York, NY: Guilford Press, 1997.

Barkley, Russell. *Taking Charge of ADHD*. New York, NY: Guilford Press, 2000.

Barkley, Russell A. *Your Defiant Child: Eight Steps to Better Behavior*. New York, NY: Guilford Press, 1998.

Baron, Ida Sue. *Neuropsychological Evaluation of the Child*. Oxford: Oxford University Press, 2004.

Bashe, Patricia Romanowski, Barbara L. Kirby, Simon Baron-Cohen, and Tony Attwood. *The OASIS Guide to Asperger Syndrome: Completely Revised and Updated: Advice, Support, Insight, and Inspiration*. New York, NY: Crown (Random House), 2005.

Braaten, Ellen, and Gretchen Felopulos. *Straight Talk about Psychological Testing for Kids*. New York, NY: Guilford Press, 2004.

Brooks, Robert. "The Search for Islands of Competence: A Metaphor of Hope and Strength," Available at URL: http://www.drrobertbrooks.com/writings/ articles/0506.html; http://www.drrobertbrooks.com.

Brown, Thomas E. *Attention Deficit Disorder: The Unfocused Mind in Children and Adults*. New Haven, CT: Yale University Press, 2005.

Channon, Shelley, Polly Pratt, and Mary M. Robertson. "Executive Function, Memory, and Learning in Tourette's Syndrome." *Neuropsychology, 17(2)* (2003), 247-254.

Cooper-Kahn, Joyce, and Laurie Dietzel, "Why Can't This Child Get Organized? Building Competence in Disorganized Kids," In the *Program Book for CHADD's 17th Annual International Conference on Attention-Deficit/Hyperactivity Disorder*, 211-214, Dallas, TX, October 2005.

Culhane-Shelburne, Kathleen, Lynn Chapieski, Merrill Hiscock, and Daniel Glaze. "Executive Functions in Children with Frontal and Temporal Lobe Epilepsy." *Journal of the International Neuropsychological Society, 8(5)* (2002), 623-632.

Dawson, Peg, and Richard Guare. *Executive Skills in Children and Adolescents: A Practical Guide to Assessment and Intervention*. New York, NY: Guilford Press, 2004.

Denckla, Martha Bridge. "Binding Together the Definitions of Attention-Deficit/Hyperactivity Disorder and Learning Disabilities," in *Executive Function in Education: From Theory to Practice,* edited by Lynn Meltzer, 5-18. New York, NY: Guilford Press, 2007.

Denckla, Martha Bridge. "Executive Function, the Overlap Zone between Attention Deficit Hyperactivity Disorder and Learning Disabilities." *International Pediatrics, 4(2)* (1989), 155-160.

Dendy, Chris A. Zeigler. *Teenagers with ADD and ADHD: A Guide for Parents and Professional, 2nd ed.* Bethesda, MD: Woodbine House, 2006.

Dendy, Chris A. Zeigler. "Understanding the Link Between Executive Functions and School Success." *Attention! Magazine* (Feb. 2008): 18-21.

Diamond, Marian, and Janet Hopson. *Magic Trees of the Mind: How to Nurture Your Child's Intelligence, Creativity, and Healthy Emotions from Birth Through Adolescence.* New York, NY: Penguin, 1999.

Eliot, Lise. *What's Going on in There?: How the Brain and Mind Develop in the First Five Years of Life.* New York, NY: Bantam Books (1999).

Federici, Ronald S. *Help for the Hopeless Child: A Guide for Families (With Special Discussion for Assessing and Treating the Post-Institutionalized Child), 2nd ed.* Alexandria, VA: Ronald S. Federici and Associates, 2001.

Frender, Gloria. *Learning to Learn: Strengthening Study Skills and Brain Power, Revised ed.* Nashville: Incentive, 2004.

Giedd, Jay N. "Structural Magnetic Resonance Imaging of the Adolescent Brain." *Annals of the New York Academy of Science, 1021* (2004): 77-85.

Gioia, Gerard A., Peter K. Isquith, Lauren Kenworthy, and Richard M. Barton. "Profiles of Everyday Executive Function in Acquired and Developmental Disorders." *Child Neuropsychology, 8(2)* (2002), 121-137.

Gioia, Gerard A., Peter K. Isquith, Steven C. Guy, and Lauren Kenworthy. *Behavior Rating Inventory of Executive Function, Professional Manual.* Odessa, FL: Psychological Assessment Resources, 2000.

Gioia, Gerard A., and Peter K. Isquith. "New Perspectives on Educating Children with ADHD: Contributions of the Executive Functions." *Journal of Health Care Law & Policy, 5* (2002), 124-163.

Goldberg, Donna, and Jennifer Zweibel. *The Organized Student: Teaching Children the Skills for Success in School and Beyond.* New York, NY: Simon & Schuster (Fireside), 2005.

Goldberg, Elkhonon. *The Executive Brain: Frontal Lobes and the Civilized Mind.* Oxford: Oxford University Press, 2001.

Greene, Ross W. *The Explosive Child: A New Approach for Understanding and Parenting Easily Frustrated, Chronically Inflexible Children.* New York, NY: HarperCollins, 1998.

Hallowell, Edward M., and John J. Ratey, *Delivered From Distraction: Getting the Most Out of Life with Attention Deficit Disorder.* New York, NY: Random House, 2005.

Healy, Jane. *Your Child's Growing Mind: Brain Development and Learning from Birth to Adolescence, 3rd ed.* New York, NY: Broadway Books (Random House), 2004.

Hill, Elizabeth L. "Executive Dysfunction in Autism." *TRENDS in Cognitive Sciences, 8(1)* (2004), 26-32.

Kelley, Mary L. *School-Home Notes: Promoting Children's Classroom Success.* New York, NY: Guilford Press, 1990.

Klass, Perri, and Ellen Costello. *Quirky Kids: Understanding and Helping Your Child Who Doesn't Fit In - When to Worry and When Not to Worry.* New York, NY: Random House, 2003.

Kleinhans, Natalia, Natacha Akshoomoff, and Dean C. Delis. "Executive Functions in Autism and Asperger's Disorder: Flexibility, Fluency, and Inhibition." *Developmental Neuropsychology, 27(3)* (2005), 379-401.

Levine, Mel. *A Mind at a Time.* New York, NY: Simon & Schuster, 2002.

Levine, Mel. *The Myth of Laziness.* New York, NY: Simon & Schuster, 2003.

Lyon, G. Reid, and Norman A. Krasgenor, eds. *Attention, Memory, and Executive Function.* Baltimore, MD: Paul H. Brookes, 1996.

Meltzer, Lynn, ed. *Executive Function in Education: From Theory to Practice.* New York, NY: Guilford Press, 2007.

MTA Cooperative Group. "A Fourteen-Month Randomized Clinical Trial of Treatment Strategies for Attention-Deficit/Hyperactivity Disorder." *Archives of General Psychiatry, 56* (1999), 1073-1086.

Nadeau, Kathleen G. *Help4ADD@High School.* Silver Spring, MD: Advantage Books, 1998.

Nadeau, Kathleen G., Ellen B. Littman, and Patricia O. Quinn. *Understanding Girls with AD/HD.* Silver Spring, MD: Advantage Books, 2000.

Naglieri, Jack A. and Eric B. Pickering. *Helping Children Learn: Intervention Handouts for Use in School and at Home.* Baltimore, MD: Paul H. Brookes, 2003.

Nigg, Joel T. *What Causes ADHD?: Understanding What Goes Wrong and Why.* New York, NY: Guilford Press, 2006.

Olivier, Carolyn, Rosemary F. Bowler, and Bill Cosby. *Learning to Learn.* New York, NY: Simon & Schuster, 1996.

Owens, Judith, et al. "Television-viewing Habits and Sleep Disturbance in School Children." *Pediatrics* [electronic article], *104(3):e27* (1999). Available at URL: http://pediatrics.aappublications.org/cgi/content/full/104/3/e27.

Pavuluri, Mani, et al. "Neurocognitive Function in Unmedicated Manic and Medicated Euthymic Pediatric Bipolar Patients." *American Journal of Psychiatry, 163* (2006), 286-293.

Pennington, Bruce F. "Dimensions of Executive Functions in Normal and Abnormal Development," in *Development of the Prefrontal Cortex: Evolution, Neurobiology, and Behavior,* edited by Norman A. Krasgenor, G. Reid Lyon, and Patricia S. Goldman-Rakic, 265-281. Baltimore, MD: Paul H. Brookes, 1997.

Phelan, Thomas W. *1-2-3 Magic: Effective Discipline for Children 2-12, 3rd ed.* Glen Ellyn, IL: Parentmagic, Inc., 2004.

Quinn, Patricia O., and Judith M. Stern. *Putting on the Brakes: Young People's Guide to Understanding Attention Deficit Hyperactivity Disorder.* Washington, DC: Magination Press, 2001.

Reiter, Astrid, Oliver Tucha, and Klaus W. Lange. "Executive Functions in Children with Dyslexia." *Dyslexia, 11(2)* (2005), 116-131.

Rich, Brendan A., et al. "Different Psychophysiological and Behavioral Responses Elicited by Frustration in Pediatric Bipolar Disorder and Severe Mood Dysregulation." *American Journal of Psychiatry, 164(2)* (2007), 309-317.

Rooney, Karen. *Independent Strategies for Efficient Study.* Richmond, VA: J.R. Enterprises, 1990.

Rourke, Byron P., ed. *Syndrome of Nonverbal Learning Disabilities: Neurodevelopmental Manifestations.* New York, NY: Guilford Press, 1995.

Shallice, Tim, et al. "Executive Function Profile of Children with Attention Deficit Hyperactivity Disorder." *Developmental Neuropsychology, 21(1)* (2002), 43-71.

Siegel, Daniel J. *The Developing Mind: How Relationships and the Brain Interact to Shape Who We Are.* New York, NY: Guilford Press, 2001.

Stevens, Suzanne. *Enabling Disorganized Students To Succeed.* Winston-Salem, NC: The Learning Development Network, 1987.

Stien, Phyllis T., and Joshua C. Kendall. *Psychological Trauma and the Developing Brain.* New York, NY: Haworth Press, 2004.

Strauch, Barbara, *The Primal Teen: What the New Discoveries About the Teenage Brain Tell Us About Our Kids*. New York, NY: Random House, 2003.

Tanguay, Pamela E., and Byron P. Rourke. *Nonverbal Learning Disabilities at Home: A Parent's Guide*. London: Jessica Kingsley Publishers, 2001.

Walker, Beth. *The Girls' Guide to AD/HD: Don't Lose This Book!* Bethesda, MD: Woodbine House, 2004.

Weinfeld, Rich, Sue Jeweler, Linda Barnes-Robinson, and Betty Shevitz. *Smart Kids with Learning Difficulties: Overcoming Obstacles and Realizing Potential*. Austin, TX: Prufrock Press, 2006.

Wright, Peter W.D., and Pamela Darr Wright. *Wrightslaw: From Emotions to Advocacy: The Special Education Survival Guide, 2nd ed.* Hartfield, VA: Harbor House Law Press, 2006.

Zelazo, Philip David, and Ulrich Müeller. "Executive Function in Typical and Atypical Development." In *Handbook of Childhood Cognitive Development*, edited by Usha Goswami, 445-469. Oxford: Blackwell, 2002.

Index

Page numbers in italics indicate tables of figures.

About the Authors

Joyce Cooper-Kahn, Ph.D., is a clinical child psychologist and co-founder of Psychological Resource Associates, a private mental health group in Severna Park, Maryland, where she specializes in helping children and families to successfully manage the variety of developmental challenges affecting children. Dr. Cooper-Kahn has particular expertise in learning and attention disorders. She holds a doctorate in clinical psychology from Catholic University and earned her undergraduate degree from Barnard College. She is the parent of an adult son with AD/HD and executive skills weaknesses.

Laurie C. Dietzel, Ph.D., is a clinical psychologist with expertise in neuropsychological assessment and the diagnosis of ADHD, learning disabilities, PDD, and other neurodevelopmental disorders. Following her undergraduate work at the University of Vermont, Dr. Dietzel earned her Ph.D. from the University of Maryland, College Park and completed a postdoctoral fellowship in neuropsychology at the Kennedy Krieger Institute. She is currently in private practice in Silver Spring, Maryland at Dietzel Butler & Associates and provides national continuing education workshops.